HOW TO SHOW YOUR DOG AND WIN

FRANKLIN WATTS/NEW YORK/LONDON/1976

BY KURT UNKELBACH

FOR JOHN RENDEL

Illustrations by George de Lyra

Photographs courtesy of: Evelyn M. Shafer: pp. 8, 19, 26, 27, 30, 31, 34, 35, 36, 40, 52, 62, 63, 73, 84, 96, 97, 98, 99, 116, 126; United Press International: pp. 22, 49, 102, 130; ASPCA Photo by Warren McSpadden: p. 68; Mr. and Mrs. Doumaux: p. 81.

Library of Congress Cataloging in Publication Data

Unkelbach, Kurt.
How to show your dog and win.

Bibliography: p.
Includes index.
SUMMARY: Introduces the world of the dog show with information on breeds, judging, classes, and preparing and training dogs.
1. Dogs—Showing—Juvenile literature. 2. Dog shows—Juvenile literature. [1. Dogs—Showing. 2. Dog shows] I. Title.
SF425.U55 636.7'08'88 75–40179
ISBN 0–531–02622–1

5 4 3 2 1

CONTENTS

BOOKS BY KURT UNKELBACH

Uncle Charlie's Poodle

The American Book of Dogs

Love on a Leash

Those Lovable Retrievers

The Winning of Westminster

Albert Payson Terhune:
The Master of Sunnybank

Murphy

Ruffian: International Champion

The Pleasure of Dog Ownership
[with Evie Unkelbach]

The Dog in My Life

The Dog Who Never Knew

How to Make Money in Dogs

How to Bring Up Your Pet Dog

Both Ends of the Leash

You're a Good Dog, Joe

A Cat and His Dogs

Catnip

Tiger Up a Tree

HOW TO SHOW YOUR DOG AND WIN

5
WINNERS
SHAFER PHOTO

INTRODUCING THE DOG GAME: WHERE THE ACTION IS

Jim Elliot is seventeen years old, and I envy his bank account. He has put enough money aside to pay for most of his college education. I call his money-making a business, but Jim insists that it's only a hobby, and the "hobby" is dogs.

It all started when Jim was seven and declared that all he wanted for Christmas was "one of those spotted dogs." Santa Claus cooperated, and there was a Dalmatian pup under the tree on Christmas morning. The runt of his litter, Bingo had had a price tag of only twenty-five dollars. As a neighbor, I was able to watch this pup mature into a handsome dog, and it seemed to me that he was just as good as the Dalmatians who were winning at the dog shows.

Jim's parents were unimpressed by my thinking, but the boy was intrigued, and he accompanied me to a few dog shows. What we saw confirmed my thinking, and he was pleased to note that children of his own age were handling their dogs in the breed ring, where canine championships are made. The sport of showing dogs looked like fun to Jim, and he started training Bingo in the breed ring routine. Six months and nine shows later, Bingo was a champion.

By then, Dalmatian breeders had seen the dog, been impressed, and used him at stud. Within two years, Champion Bingo's stud fee had jumped from $100 to $300. Today, Bingo isn't as active as he used to be, but a champion son of his commands a $250 stud fee. In addition, Jim owns three Dalmatian bitches. Their pups are priced from $150 to $250.

All five of his adult Dalmatians live in the house. Outdoors, there's a small kennel (a converted tool shed) for bitches in season and pups. Jim tells me that many of his friends think he's crazy for being so involved with dogs, but he can laugh all the way to the bank, and has plenty of time for studies, sports, and other interests. And if he felt like it, Jim could laugh over the fact that he's miles ahead of most of his high school peers in terms of responsibility, sportsmanship, and courtesy. And he knows how to make new friends, how to act in public, and how to enjoy one's dog. Along the way, of course, Jim has learned a great deal about dogs in general and Dalmatians in particular.

But what if one essential fact had been different? What if Bingo had been of such poor quality that he could not have won his championship in the breed ring? My hunch is that Jim would have entered his spotted dog in the other two sports found at dog shows: Junior Showmanship and Obedience. In those sports, he would have learned more about dogs and enhanced the development of his own personality. And since he's always been a thrifty young man, it's rational to assume that he would have banked Bingo's winnings and used the loot to purchase a quality pup. In the long run, then, Jim would have ended up as he is today: a dog fancier and a successful breeder.

Dog fancier? That term applies to any dog lover who has a reputation for more canine expertise than the average dog lover. All it really takes to earn that reputation is a little personal ambition and one purebred dog over the age of six months. The dog must belong to one of the 129 breeds recognized or listed by the American Kennel Club, but you don't have to own the dog. You can co-own him with another person, or he can belong to a member of your family: father, mother, sister, brother, uncle, or aunt.

There are two types of dog fanciers: purist and opportunist. The purist is content with owning winning dogs and filling up the empty spaces in his trophy cabinet, while the opportunist looks around for ways to turn his knowledge of dogs into dollars. Among the young dog fanciers whom I know, Jim is the ranking opportunist. Others earn anything from pin money to a healthy weekly income by training dogs for owners who lack either the time or intelligence to train, by baby sitting for beloved pooches, by exercising the pets of shut-ins, and by trimming canine nails. Several earn steady money by running small boarding kennels. An owner pays several dollars a day to board a dog, but the dog's daily upkeep amounts to pennies. There will always be a shortage of good, reliable boarding kennels in this country, and a shortage of something else, too: people who know how to clip and groom a poodle. About 30 percent of the purebreds in this country are poodles, but 80 percent of their owners don't know how to take care of the breed's coat. In my neck of the woods, two sisters —one twelve and the other fifteen—are operating a poodle beauty parlor in their spare time. They learned the hard way, by preparing their own poodles for the dog shows.

In the dog game, dog shows are where the action is, and that's what this book is all about: how to win with your dog in the breed ring, or Junior Showmanship, or Obedience—or all three. Only at the shows can you gain recognition as a dog fancier and earn the right to wear the mysterious halo that distinguishes you from the average dog lover. If your dog wins big, as Bingo did, the halo becomes bigger and the rep comes faster. But win or lose, the rep does come. Locally at first, and then it spreads, as the press and the canine journals pick up the names of you and your dog.

There's fun and excitement at the dog shows, to say nothing of the chance to win prizes, trophies, and a measure of fame. Thousands of dog lovers become new dog fanciers every year, and once involved, they find the dog fancy hard to shake. In a sense, the fancy is controlled by a harmless, fascinating disease that I like to call *canis feveritis familis.* Once it hits you, it usually spreads to other members of your family, and they become involved. When this happens, the whole family finds a community of interest in dogs. Fathers and mothers forget bridge clubs, and brothers and sisters drop out of such popular activities as taking dope, drag racing, and burning down school buildings.

Enough! We are gathered here to discuss the wonderful world of dog shows and the sports that world offers to you and your pet dog.

THE WONDERFUL WORLD OF DOG SHOWS

Laymen, dog haters, and cat lovers often display their innocence by referring to dog shows as canine beauty contests. But they are not that and they never were. Who, in his right mind, would call a bulldog a beautiful animal? Or a pug? Or an affenpinscher?

In this country, dog shows had their beginnings in the years that followed the Civil War. They were instituted by breeders who were anxious to compare their dogs with those of other breeders, and thus learn what progress they were making. The shows were dedicated to the improvement of the breeds, and this spirit prevailed for a long time. Most of the breeders were ladies and gentlemen of considerable wealth, owners of large kennels who thought nothing of showing twenty dogs at a show. Let us be grateful. They stamped the showing of dogs as a sporting activity.

For sportsmen who liked to shoot, it was a time of plenty. Our waters were crowded with ducks and geese, and our woods and fields teemed with upland birds. Since market hunters dominated the waterfowl scene, sportsmen turned to the upland birds, and that's why the only purebred dogs found at those early, informal dog shows were setters, pointers, and spaniels. The spaniels were in the minority.

The first formal dog show ever held in this country took place in June of 1874 and was sponsored by the Illinois State Sportsmen's Association. The site was Chicago, the sporting breeds predominated, and all the owners went home in a happy frame of mind. The judges didn't rank the dogs in a given class, so no prizes were given, and there were no losers. The judges merely commented on the strong features of each dog.

Despite the lack of decisions, the show was a huge success in that it attracted over five thousand ticket-buying spectators. The crowd inspired other dog-loving groups, and within three years other annual dog shows were launched in Detroit, Saint Louis, Memphis, Columbus, Bridgeport, Paris (Kentucky), and Mineola (New York).

Judging was at the class level. There were classes for both adults and puppies, and usually males and bitches of a given breed were judged separately, so there were four classes per breed. At some shows, each class was further divided into two classes: one for American-breds, the other for imported dogs. A single breed, then, could have as many as eight classes.

Of all those early shows, only one remains: the annual show sponsored by the Westminster Kennel Club. The club staged its first show in 1877, and 1975 marked its ninety-ninth consecutive year. Because of space limitations, Westminster—held each February in Madison Square Garden, New York City—is confined to 3,000 dogs, with the further limitation that each of them must have earned at least one championship point to be eligible. While it is no longer the biggest dog show in the country, it is the oldest one in the world, and still tops in importance to most exhibitors. An ardent dog fancier considers his life misspent if one of his dogs (over the years) fails to win at Westminster.

In view of the fact that all of the early shows had different sets of rules and regulations, it's a small miracle that dog shows survived. The miracle was the founding of the American Kennel Club in 1884, or just in the nick of time to avert disaster in the dog fancy. Dedicated to the "advancement of purebred dogs," the AKC has become the governing body of U.S. dogdom, and is responsible (among other things) for adopting the rules and regulations that apply to all of our dog shows.

Back in 1884, the new group's founders had some sense of direction from across the Atlantic. England, land of the world's first dog show (1859), was in the midst of a purebred dog boom. Much of the credit belonged to the Kennel Club, dogdom's first national governing body, founded in 1873. Under the KC, Britain's dog game was thriving. The shows were under control, and the sport of showing dogs was rated as highly respectable by royalty, the upper classes, and the general public.

Something similar to the KC was needed in this country. The need inspired a meeting of ten very prominent American dog fanciers, all determined to form some sort of a ruling body for the dog game on these shores. They came up with the National Bench Show Association, a host of rules and regulations, and then a change of name to the American Kennel Club. To this day, there are those who insist that American Kennel Association would have been a better name. The claim has some logic. Unlike the KC, whose members have always been people, the AKC members have always been clubs.

The first members were all-breed kennel clubs from New York, Rhode Island, Connecticut, and Texas. They were outnumbered by specialty (one-breed) clubs, devoted to the fox terrier, beagle, bulldog, French bulldog, bull terrier, Boston terrier, dachshund, Irish setter, and Saint Bernard. The going wasn't easy. By 1900, there were only sixteen member clubs, but their shows were the only ones held in high esteem by serious breeders and fanciers. A dog registration system was going strong, new show classes and a championship point formula had been introduced, judges had (for the first time) some breed standards to guide their decisions, and numerous rules regarding dogs and owners were being enforced. Slowly but surely, American dog shows were settling into uniformity. New kennel and specialty clubs would spring up all over the map, and most would apply for AKC membership.

From the start, all important AKC matters were decided by majority vote. The voters were the member clubs, each entitled to a single vote and each represented by a delegate. In a very real sense, the delegates were the American dog fancy's congress, and congress sat quarterly at AKC headquarters in New York City. The governing body's constitution called for every delegate to be a man, and for a long time hardly anybody questioned this strange discrimination. Then, this side of 1930, women started to dominate the dog game. Today, they outnumber men as breeders, owners, and exhibitors, and they are among the best of our professional handlers and breed judges.

It is a pleasure to report that full and equal rights for women won AKC approval in 1974, and we already have several women as delegates. There will be many more in the future, and that's the way it should be. At the club level, women are far more active than men, occupy most of the elected offices, and carry the heavy share of the work. The AKC now boasts of more than four hundred member clubs, and an equal number of nonmember clubs. The latter are AKC all the way in spirit, but they do not vote.

In the first few decades of the AKC, new canine breeds arrived in this country in a bewildering stream. New to America, that is. Most came from England, and almost every one found immediate favor here. There was a big demand for their pups, and buyers could hardly wait for their beloved pets to reach the required minimum age for showing. It was six months in those days, and it still is in these days. Back then, insofar as quality was concerned, the new owners usually didn't know what they were buying. There were very few authorities per breed in this country, and there were none on some of the breeds. Almost always, the new dog fancier found the nearest approximation to a breed authority in that breed's judge at the nearest dog show.

In that age of innocence and enthusiasm, the AKC was moving ahead on most fronts, but not toward control of the judges. Things rolled along on an invitational basis: the show-giving club invited its own judges, with no questions asked from above. Presumably, the judges knew all there was to know about a given breed or breeds, but they didn't have to prove their qualifications beyond convincing the club's officers. If they owned dogs, conversed knowingly and rapidly, were acquainted with the right people, and seemed to be gentlemen, they were as qualified to judge as the next man, who might know a great deal more about the breeds and be able to prove it.

Some of the clubs imported a judge or two. It was a sure way to attract large entries, for American dog fanciers were awed by their counterparts in England and willingly accepted British judges as the world's best. The visitors from abroad demanded and received very high fees, plus sufficient funds to cover travel and other expenses. And it was not unusual for a British judge to arrive with several dogs. Not for showing, but for selling. The show where he judged became his salesroom. Price tags up to ten thousand dollars per canine were not unusual.

Such profiteering was not considered unethical. Since there were no preventive AKC rules, some judges couldn't resist the temptation to make money on the side in the dog game, while others considered it beneath their dignity. The latter were usually in the minority.

It's questionable if the sport of showing dogs could have survived too many judges with the wide range of activities credited to James Mortimer, one of the first big names in the American dog fancy. He started in purebred dogs a century ago, first as a breeder of bulldogs, then of rough collies and pointers, and finally of a scattering of terrier breeds. And he handled his dogs at our earliest shows, where he sold his pups, charmed the right people, and earned a reputation as a canine authority. Soon he was receiving and accepting invitations to judge. By the time the AKC was founded, Mr. Mortimer was a very popular judge of all breeds, some of them recently imported and thus new to him.

Mr. Mortimer kept extending his activities. He was hired to superintend dog shows, and to manage the kennels of wealthy dog fanciers. He also trained and handled dogs, imported and sold dogs, and acted as agent for both clubs and individuals. In addition, Judge Mortimer was a big wheel at the AKC, and, as one of the incorporators of the charter, he helped frame the constitution.

For thirty years, this man harvested profits from almost every facet of the dog game. And yet, very few people complained about the way he juggled his conflicting interests. He wasn't the only judge making hay on the side, and neither he nor the others were breaking any rules. There were no AKC rules to break.

That state of affairs was remedied after the First World War, when a new crop of dog fanciers decided that some judges needed to have their wings clipped. Golden rules for judges were proclaimed, and ever since, they have not been permitted to "trade or traffic in dogs as a means of livelihood in whole or in part." A few scoundrels do find ways to get around that ruling, but they risk losing their judgeships if discovered.

Once the AKC got around to regulating breed judges, a system for qualifying new judges went into play. This has been refined over the years, and today an applicant must prove on paper and in action that he or she is truly qualified to judge a breed or breeds. In the dog game, the honored ones are known as *licensed* judges. Technically, *approved* judges is the proper term.

It also took several decades of trial and error to refine the procedure whereby canine champions achieve their titles. A ten-point system was introduced in 1900, but it did not prove equitable for every breed, and changes were made as the years rolled by. The end result was a more complex fifteen-point system instituted in 1924 that is still current, although a couple of refinements have been added. The system is fair and square, in that it gives good dogs of any recognized AKC breed a shot at winning their championships. As careful readers will learn in chapter 3, the less popular breeds are no longer left out in the cold. It's a little more difficult for them to achieve championship status, but they can get there—so long as their owners do not lose heart.

For our purposes, the modern era of dog shows started in the late 1920s. The wealthy set no longer dominated the scene. While its members were still going strong, more and more average dog lovers—the owners of just one or two dogs—had joined the action. It was no longer necessary to maintain a large kennel and show twenty dogs at a clip in order to win big. And in 1929, the year of the big crash on Wall Street, many of the leading kennels went down the drain. Overnight, they had become luxuries, and their owners could no longer afford them.

Newcomers joined the sport in droves, and the Depression years of the 1930s failed to dent their enthusiasm. There were more shows, better roads leading to them, and more automobiles with husband and wife on the front seat and their show dog on the back seat. Those new dog fanciers came from every walk of life, and they turned dog shows into truly democratic events. It cost only a few dollars to show a dog. Maybe that's why the sport continued to progress while the nation's economy slumped.

In that same time span, two new dog show sports started to emerge. The one now known as Junior Showmanship (JS) was originated by Colonel Frank Foster Davis, famous in the dog game as an all 'rounder, or a judge of all breeds. He had long been aware that every dog show attracted many spectators who didn't understand what the heck was going on in the breed rings. Since they had paid the price of admission, wouldn't it be nice for them if they could watch at least one event that they could understand?

The benevolent judge dreamed up such an event and called it Children's Handling. He introduced it at the Pasadena Kennel Club show in 1929. The participants were a dozen children, each handling a purebred dog of a different breed. Colonel Davis judged the event. For the first time in dog show history, the winner in the show ring was a human being. The object of the new sport was to find the best handler and not the best dog.

This innovation did not make any headlines, and the whole idea almost disappeared into limbo. It was rescued by the newly formed Professional Handlers Association and revived at several Eastern shows in 1933. For a long time, Children's Handling was regarded as an informal sport, but it didn't fade away. Year after year, more shows adopted it and finally the AKC blessed it with a set of uniform rules and regulations. Junior Showmanship is now the sport's name, and it really is a better fit. The age range for competitors is ten through sixteen, and a fifteen- or sixteen-year-old handler can't be blamed for not wanting to be classified as a child. It's easier to take being rated as a junior. The lowdown on JS is up ahead in chapter 5.

The other emerging sport was (and remains) Obedience. The Big O amounts to a test of canine intelligence, and dogs prove their brilliance by going through a series of prescribed exercises under the direction of their handlers, who work with vocal commands, hand signals, or both. Unlike a show dog, a top Obedience dog never finds a championship at the end of the rainbow. In Obedience, the dogs shoot for honorary degrees. Their good looks (*conformation*) are no more important than the beauty or hand-

Of all modern breeds, the samoyed is closest to the primitive dog. This handsome specimen has just won the highest possible honor at the breed level.

BEST
OF
WINNERS
SHAFER PHOTO

someness of their handlers. Dog and handler must communicate and must operate as a team, and much more so than in the breed ring. That fact should put to rest the myth that Obedience dogs are smarter than their handlers. At the very least, the handlers have to be as intelligent as their dogs.

This newest of the dog game's sports was designed and developed in England. Although known here, it did not excite interest until Mrs. Whitehouse Walker, a leading poodle breeder, decided that the sport was just what the doctor ordered for America's dog lovers. According to the Walker Theory, Obedience was perfect for those owners who wanted to prove that their champion dogs had brains as well as beauty, or who wanted maximum pleasure at minimum expense. Such owners, of course, had to end up with well-trained dogs.

Mrs. Walker and a small band of enthusiasts and their dogs introduced the sport to America in 1934. Since AKC approval was not in hand, the early Obedience trials were listed as exhibitions. Two such exhibitions were held in 1934, there were six more in 1935 and an amazing seventeen in 1936 before the AKC was convinced and adopted the sport. Many dog fanciers argue that this is the only dog show sport that makes any sense. It is certainly the only one that offers a canine the chance to prove its potential as the complete, obedient companion of man. Check out chapter 6 for the nitty gritty on Obedience.

Right here, it's time for a review. As whelped, or in order of arrival on the American scene, these three sports comprise the world of dog shows:

1. Breed ring. In breed ring, a dog usually wins all of its championship points by proving its superiority over competing dogs of its breed in terms of conformation (body structure) and temperament.
2. Junior Showmanship. In Junior Showmanship, breed ring rules are reversed, and the handlers—not the dogs—are judged in terms of expertness and finesse.
3. Obedience. In Obedience, a dog wins canine degrees, and proves both its intelligence and the training talents of its handler.

In both breed ring and Obedience, there are no age ranges for handlers. So long as children (of any age) can control their dogs, they can handle said dogs in both sports. Junior Showmanship is limited to handlers between the ages of ten and sixteen.

If you are within the JS age limits, all three of the dog game's sports are open to you and your purebreds, granted that they qualify. And all three are found at most AKC dog shows.

Those shows are found at two levels: major (point) and minor (match), and this is the way they shape up:

MAJOR LEAGUE: THE POINT SHOW. The point show is the one that will eventually mean most to you—the show where your dog can win points toward its championship, or legs on its Obedience degree, or where you (as its handler) can score an important Open win in Junior Showmanship.

Most point shows are designated as *all-breed,* meaning that dogs of all breeds recognized or listed by the AKC may be entered. Then there are *breed specialty* shows, limited to one breed (for example, boxer), or the varieties of a breed (collie: rough and smooth). A breed specialty may be held separately or within the framework of an all-breed show. And then there are a few *group specialty* shows, limited to all the breeds of a given group, such as a *toy specialty* for the seventeen breeds in the toy group. A group specialty usually goes it alone.

About fourteen hundred point shows are held every year, and every one is designated as being benched or unbenched. At a benched show, the dogs are stationed (benched) on display platforms until a specified hour, so that spectators may have a chance to see all of the dogs at the show. At an unbenched show, a dog who is not a winner is free to leave as soon as its breed has been judged. Thus, the owners of all losing dogs have the option of getting an early start for home. Over the last three decades, the number of benched shows has declined in a hurry. In 1974, fewer than a dozen were left.

MINOR LEAGUE: THE MATCH SHOW. The match show is designed for both newcomers to the dog game and new dogs. It follows the general pattern of a point show and may be considered a modified, informal version. But while wins are rewarded, the wins do not count for points. It is here, at the minor league level, that both handlers and dogs can get the experience of working together as

a team and condition themselves for the big time of the point shows.

Putting a few match shows under one's belt before heading for the point shows is always a good idea. The shows are unbenched, the proceedings are organized but casual, and—since there's nothing to lose—there's no pressure. If he had any say in the matter, any rational show dog would plead for more experience at the match shows.

Fortunately, most match shows feature all three of the dog game's sports. Some drop the minimum age for pups from six to four months. That's a little young for the pup who is not overly aggressive. At four months, the average pup is still pretty much of a baby, and is just starting to lose his baby teeth. The grand total of match shows is now about thirty-five hundred per annum.

Point shows and match shows are held in all seasons of the year, indoors or outdoors, and in every state. Almost all of the point shows are one-day events. Most match shows run from noon to dusk, although some are staged in the evening.

Wherever you live, you'll find numerous match shows and a satisfactory number of point shows within easy driving distance every year. In the old days, all point shows were held on weekends. Today, to avoid conflicts in a given area, they are also held on weekdays and holidays. Thus far, only Christmas has remained immune, but don't take bets on how long that day will be safe.

A win for one's dog on December 25? Tens of thousands of dog fanciers would consider that the greatest Christmas present of all time. Blame *canis feveritis*.

Five-year-old Erik Williamson may not be ready to handle his pet keeshond, but that does not prevent him from enjoying the Best of Breed trophy won by the dog at a recent specialty show. The keeshond is a non-sporting breed with thick, silver-gray hair.

THE BREEDS

Researchers, statisticians, and others concerned with numbers estimate the number of pure breeds running around in the world today at anywhere from four hundred to seven hundred. Educated guessers are content with the lower figure, since that's close to the total number of breeds recognized by all of the worlds' kennel clubs. Insofar as the American dog game is concerned, the true grand total is unimportant. Here, the only breeds that count are the ones eligible for action at the dog shows.

These breeds now total 129. The big majority, or 121 (a few with varieties), are *recognized* by the American Kennel Club. They are the only breeds that may become AKC champions of record, a fact of life that sets them apart and on high from the 8 minority breeds. The latter are known as *listed,* or *miscellaneous,* breeds. While the AKC permits them to compete in the show ring, they cannot become champions and can win only ribbons, prizes, trophies, and fame.

For show purposes, the AKC has divided the recognized breeds into six groups. As we'll learn on future pages, this brings order to a many-faceted event, saves time, and assures steady progress toward a rational climax. In general, all the breeds assigned to a group represent the same original purpose or current status in life.

Sporting Group. Breeds developed to find and retrieve game from land and/or water; *game* is defined as upland birds and waterfowl.

Pointer
Pointer, German shorthaired
Pointer, German wirehaired
Retriever, Chesapeake Bay
Retriever, curly-coated
Retriever, flat-coated
Retriever, golden
Retriever, Labrador
Setter, English
Setter, Gordon
Setter, Irish
Spaniel, American water
Spaniel, Brittany
Spaniel, Clumber
Spaniel, cocker:
  Solid color, black
  ASCOB (any solid color other than black, to include black-and-tan)
  Parti-color
Spaniel, English cocker
Spaniel, English springer
Spaniel, field
Spaniel, Irish water
Spaniel, Sussex
Spaniel, Welsh springer
Vizsla
Weimaraner
Wirehaired pointing griffon

Hound Group. Breeds developed to track, trail, and run down game, or to hold same at bay; *game* is defined as wild and four-footed.

Afghan hound
Basenji

Above: Irish setter
(sporting group)

Right: Beagle
(hound group)

Basset hound

Beagle:

Not exceeding thirteen inches in height

Over thirteen and not exceeding fifteen inches in height

Bloodhound

Borzoi

Coonhound, black and tan

Dachshund:

Longhaired

Smooth

Wirehaired

Foxhound, American

Foxhound, English

Greyhound

Harrier

Irish wolfhound

Norwegian elkhound

Otter hound

Rhodesian ridgeback

Saluki

Scottish deerhound

Whippet

WORKING GROUP. Breeds developed as nonsalaried labor for such purposes as hauling, herding, guarding, and guiding.

Akita

Alaskan Malamute

Belgian Malinois

Belgian sheepdog

Belgian Tervuren

Bernese mountain dog

Bouvier des Flandres

Boxer

Briard

Bull mastiff

Collie:

Rough

Smooth

Doberman pinscher
German shepherd dog
Giant schnauzer
Great Dane
Great Pyrenees
Komondor (plural: Komondorok)
Kuvasz (plural: Kuvaszok)
Mastiff
Newfoundland
Old English sheepdog
Puli (plural: Pulik)
Rottweiler
Saint Bernard
Samoyed
Schnauzer, standard
Shetland sheepdog
Siberian husky
Welsh corgi, Cardigan
Welsh corgi, Pembroke

TERRIER GROUP. Breeds developed for going to earth after assorted vermin and varmints.

Airedale terrier
American Staffordshire terrier
Australian terrier
Bedlington terrier
Border terrier
Bull terrier:
  White
  Colored
Cairn terrier
Dandie Dinmont terrier
Fox terrier:
  Smooth
  Wire
Irish terrier
Kerry blue terrier
Lakeland terrier

Smooth collie
(working group)

Miniature schnauzer
(terrier group)

Manchester terrier, standard
Miniature schnauzer
Norwich terrier
Scottish terrier
Sealyham terrier
Skye terrier
Soft-coated wheaten terrier
Staffordshire bull terrier
Welsh terrier
West Highland white terrier

TOY GROUP. Breeds developed for status or spoiling.

Affenpinscher
Brussels griffon
Chihuahua:
- Long coat
- Smooth coat

English toy spaniel:
- Ruby
- King Charles
- Blenheim
- Prince Charles

Italian greyhound
Japanese spaniel
Maltese
Manchester terrier, toy
Miniature pinscher
Papillon
Pekingese
Pomeranian
Poodle, toy
Pug
Shih tzu
Silky terrier
Yorkshire terrier

NON-SPORTING GROUP. Breeds that have outlived their original purposes and really don't belong in any of the other groups.

Bichon Frise
Boston terrier
Bulldog
Chow chow
Dalmatian
French bulldog
Keeshond (plural: Keeshonden)
Lhasa apso
Poodle:
  Miniature
  Standard
Schipperke
Tibetan terrier

MISCELLANEOUS BREEDS.

Australian cattle dog
Australian kelpie
Bearded collie
Border collie
Cavalier King Charles spaniel
Ibizan hound
Miniature bull terrier
Spinone italiano

As noted in the group listings, several of the recognized breeds have varieties. A given breed's varieties reflect differences in size (poodle, beagle), or coat (collie, dachshund), or coat color (cocker spaniel, bull terrier). By approving the differences, the AKC keeps all admirers of a breed happy; to each his own preference in size, coat, or color.

For show purposes, each variety of a breed is treated as an individual breed. Thus, at an all-breed show, the winner of each variety advances to the next level of competition, or the right breed group.

As for those eight miscellaneous breeds, while they can't become champions, they are on an equal footing with the recognized breeds in the sports of Junior Showmanship and Obedience. And each is a candidate for future full recognition by the AKC. Before

Left: Shih tzu (toy group)

Above: Dalmatian (non-sporting group)

Ibizan hound
(miscellaneous)

that happy day arrives, a given breed's supporters must maintain a proper set of breeding records (a stud book) and build the breed's total population to a respectable figure. These days, a miscellaneous breed has a good chance of achieving AKC recognition when about fifteen hundred representatives are wagging tails in about thirty states.

When recognized, the honored miscellaneous breed will be assigned to an appropriate group. In the immediate future, the candidates with the best chances are the bearded collie and the Cavalier King Charles spaniel. The border collie is around in very heavy numbers, but the breed's admirers are more interested in working ability than conformation. Unless they achieve unexpected popularity, the other five breeds on the miscellaneous list have very little chance of making the grade.

In the dog game, the nearest thing to a Gallup Poll is the annual record of new dogs (mostly pups) registered by the AKC. The grand total went over the million mark for the first time in 1970. Since less than 25 percent of the purebred pups whelped every year are ever registered, it's safe to estimate that well over four million new purebred pups will help populate the United States this year.

Of all the recognized breeds, the poodle has been king of the hill for many years, and there's no reason to suspect that he won't reign for another decade or so. One out of every five purebred dogs in the United States is a poodle. The beast that comes in three sizes outnumbers the next-in-line German shepherd by two to one. Here are the top twenty popular breeds:

1. Poodle
2. German shepherd dog
3. Irish setter
4. Beagle
5. Dachshund
6. Doberman pinscher
7. Miniature schnauzer
8. Labrador retriever
9. Cocker spaniel
10. Saint Bernard
11. Collie

12. Pekingese
13. Shetland sheepdog
14. Golden retriever
15. Chihuahua
16. Great Dane
17. Brittany spaniel
18. Yorkshire terrier
19. Siberian husky
20. Lhasa apso

Since the annual count of the breeds was begun in 1926, only five breeds have occupied the top spot. For those who can't wait to learn their names:

1. German shepherd dog (1926–1928)
2. Boston terrier (1929–1935)
3. Cocker spaniel (1936–1952)
4. Beagle (1953–1959)
5. Poodle (1960–present)

Currently, the only one of those breeds not in the first ten is the Boston terrier, which is in the twenty-seventh spot and being challenged by the Afghan. This is rather sad, for the Bostonian is the only native American breed among the five. Does the breed's fall from great popularity mean that dog fanciers are not as patriotic as they were in 1935?

3

THE BREED RING

As previously noted, the dog game is home to three sports for young dog lovers. The oldest is the breed ring, a product of the nineteenth century that has been changed, amended, and refined in this century. It is here in the breed ring that show dogs compete to win the points that will earn them the title of champion. The one predictable thing about this canine sport is that even a great dog cannot become a champion by staying at home. To succeed, *the beasts must compete against other members of their breed* at the point shows, and *they must win over at least some of them.*

Let us pause and consider these two requirements. Under normal circumstances, they represent the whole of the point system for almost all of the breeds. But for a few of the least popular breeds, circumstances can be abnormal. Consider such noble purebreds as the harrier, otter hound, and Sussex spaniel. At some all-breed point shows, only one dog of the breed might be entered. Since no other members of its breed are present, the lone harrier cannot win over other harriers, nor can it win points at the breed level. Still, it's the best harrier on hand, and that doesn't have to be a hollow achievement. An opportunity to win points awaits the lonely harrier at a higher level. As we shall see, the AKC does not forget the less popular breeds.

OF
SITE
X
ER PHOTO

In the more popular breeds, about one out of every sixty show dogs becomes a champion. But these odds are not as forbidding as they seem, for many of the dogs at any given point show should have stayed at home. They are show dogs in name only, and the name was given to them by their loving owners. Other dog fanciers might well call them "bums," the term used for dogs that fall far short of their breed standard.

Love for one's dog often blinds the beholders to their dogs' defects. This is a very common affliction in the dog game, and it is called *kennel blindness*. Most of the kennel-blind fanciers whom I know are school teachers, bankers, politicians, and salesmen, and many of them are also hobby breeders of dogs.

Kennel-blind owners cannot be discouraged. They continue to spend time and money in showing their dogs, and often gain inspiration from the fact that there are some canine champions around that are bigger "bums" than their own dogs. There is sufficient evidence to prove that they are right. Every year, some undeserving dogs become champions, and this situation will continue until the AKC comes up with a way to control the minds of its licensed breed judges. No two think alike.

Every AKC breed has its own breed standard, a written blueprint that describes the ideal dog of the breed. It is the sworn duty of the breed judge to compare all dogs with their breed standards, and then to find the winner in the dog that comes closest. But this depends upon the judge's interpretation or misinterpretation of the written breed standard. Thus, every year and in every breed, "bum" dogs do become champions. They were lucky enough to go under a sufficient number of judges with wild imaginations or only vague recollections of the breed standard. Nonetheless, the great majority of champions do deserve their championships. They are called *typey* dogs, in that they come close to the type (ideal) described in the breed standards.

This elegant Afghan hound has earned high honors at the breed level.

ENTERING A POINT SHOW

Not every purebred dog or bitch belonging to one of the 121 breeds recognized by the American Kennel Club can be shown in the breed ring. To be deserving of a try for their championships, dogs must meet certain qualifications.

1. They must be registered with the AKC.
2. They must be over six months old.
3. They must not be blind(totally), deaf, vicious, or lame.
4. They must meet the specifications of their own breed standards. A white German shepherd dog, for example, usually commands a high price, but its color disqualifies it for the breed ring, since the breed standard does not permit a white coat. Ditto for a magnificent whippet, Samoyed, or bull terrier with blue eyes, which in each of these breeds is a disqualifying fault.
5. Each sex must be whole or intact—as nature intended for reproductive purposes. Thus, a dog must have both testicles in the scrotum, and a bitch cannot be spayed.
6. They cannot be changed in appearance (cropped ears, docked tail, changed natural color or markings) except as specified in their breed standards.
7. Obviously, the dogs must have four legs, two ears, two eyes, one tail, and all of their teeth.

Fortunately, the overwhelming majority of dogs in all of the 121 AKC recognized breeds meet those qualifications. The 8 AKC listed (or miscellaneous) breeds must also meet them. All of these 129 breeds are eligible to compete in the breed ring at point shows, but the listed breeds can only win ribbons or trophies—no championship points.

So, insofar as making a dog into a champion is concerned, we are dealing with only the 121 recognized breeds. Both the good ones and the poor ones are found at point shows, where the "advancement of the breeds" is now mostly spiritual. Winning is the major objective—for only winners bring home the bacon, the championship points that add up to a championship.

HOW A CHAMPIONSHIP IS EARNED

To become a titleholder, a dog or bitch must win fifteen championship points. On the other hand, it can win fifty points and still fail to make its championship. The fifteen points have to be won in the right way, in that they must include two major wins, and the dog must have won under at least three different judges. (A major win is one that scores either three, four, or five points.)

This is not as complicated as it sounds. The number of points up for grabs in each recognized breed at a point show varies from none at all to five, depending upon the number of dogs competing in the breed (and the variables of sex and geography, as we shall soon explain). Thus, a dog can win its championship at three big point shows by picking up three major wins of five points each, each under a different judge. Or, a dog can win its title by picking up two major wins of three points each, each under a different judge, plus the balance of the needed fifteen points through one- and two-point (minor) wins, with at least one of them coming under a third judge. You can handle a dog in the breed ring until it is five or six years old.

The point system varies from breed to breed. Generally, a popular breed requires that more dogs be in competition per point than a less popular breed. Thus, where thirty-four dogs might be the requirement for a three-point major in German shepherd dogs, it might only be nine dogs in pugs.

Another variable in the determination of points is sex. It can go one way or the other. At a show where it takes ten dogs (males) in competition to earn a three-point major, as in Dalmatians, it might take eleven bitches for the so-called weaker sex to win three points.

Still another variable is the geographical location of the show. The AKC provides different point schedules for four regions of the continental United States, plus other point schedules for Alaska, Hawaii, and Puerto Rico. Thus, in rough collies, it takes twenty dogs in competition to put three points up for grabs at a New York show (District 1: mostly Northern and Eastern states), but thirty-two dogs are necessary to win the same number of points in California (District 3).

All clear? At any point show, the point schedule for the area appears in the show catalog. All of the point schedules are reviewed—and sometimes revised—by the AKC on an annual basis.

THE LEVELS OF COMPETITION

A dog show is really a series of eliminations that take place on three progressive levels. To better understand it all, let's take a quick overall look at the three levels, and then go back to the beginning of the lowest level—the classes within the breeds—and work our way up.

1. The breed level. Here, through a succession of classes, all the dogs of a breed (or variety) compete until one dog wins out. This dog is Best of Breed (or Best of Variety), BOB (or BOV), and the only one of that breed (variety) eligible for further competition.
2. The group level. All of the BOB and BOV winners compete within their respective groups (see chapter 2). Thus, all of the Sporting dogs compete, and the winners of first, second, third, and fourth places are determined. But only the first-place winner of the Sporting group goes on to further competition.
3. Best-in-Show level. The six group winners compete for the title of Best in Show (BIS). This one BIS dog or bitch is the best canine present at the show, wins all sorts of loot, and shares the glory with his or her owner. To a dog fancier, owning a BIS dog is more important than being elected President. It is a grand and glorious feeling, something to remember for the rest of one's life.

Now let's take it all from the beginning and in depth.

THE BREED LEVEL

All point shows, benched or unbenched, are held in accordance with the approved AKC formula. For every registered breed, the action begins in the classes, where the sexes are judged separately, and the gentlemen are judged before the ladies. The sequence of the classes is always the same.

1. Puppy Class. Dogs must be over six months and under one year (one day short of the dog's first birthday), and whelped in the United States or Canada. Here the pups compete with their peers and have their best chance of winning. The younger the pups, the more immature they will be, and the smaller their chances against the more mature dogs usually found in the following classes.
2. Novice Class. Dogs must be six months and over and whelped in the United States or Canada. Senior pups and young adults who still need a little breed ring experience are usually found here. But dogs can't stay in this class forever. They are ineligible after winning three first prizes in Novice, or one first prize in any of the succeeding classes.
3. Bred-by-Exhibitor Class. Dogs must be six months and over and whelped in the United States, although a dog whelped in Canada is eligible if he is registered with the Canadian KC. The sticky-wicket about this class is that the dog's owner or co-owner must also be the dog's breeder or the breeder's spouse, and only members of the owner's or co-owner's immediate family are permitted to handle. In this case, immediate family means wife, husband, mother, father, son, daughter, brother, and sister. A favorite class for breeders who are bringing out their homebred prides and joys.
4. American-bred Class. Dogs must be six months and over and (obviously) whelped in the United States as a result of a mating that took place there. Owners often enter their dogs in this class to let the judge know that their dogs are true patriots and were not imported from foreign countries.
5. Open Class. Dogs must be six months and older. This is the toughest class to win, since most of the dogs have reached maturity and already have championship points to their credit. Champions can be entered here, but seldom are, since the owner of a champion hates to risk defeat by a class (nonchampion) dog. This is also the only class for dogs whelped in countries other than the United States and Canada.

If enough dogs are present in the above classes, the judge selects the best four in the class, places them from one to four, and hands out the appropriate ribbons. (Where less than four are entered in the class, he places the number competing.) The first-prize winner earns a blue ribbon, and of course this also means that the dog (including the blue-ribbon puppy) is still in the running for championship points.

All clear? Anyone who is not hep to the dog game is usually impressed by those who boast about the blue ribbons their dogs have won. Actually, a dog can be a pretty miserable representative of its breed and still win a trunkful of blue ribbons if it is shown only at small shows and seldom meets competition in its classes.

The ribbon that counts is the purple ribbon, and it goes to the winner of the Winners class.

6. Winners Class. The first-prize winners in each of the five classes return to the breed ring. The judge selects one of these dogs as the best dog present and names him Winners Dog (WD). It is one person's opinion, of course, and usually the only other person sharing it is the owner of the WD. Nonetheless, this is the dog—and the only dog—that wins the available championship points for males of his breed. If these points are fewer than five, he still has a chance to add to his total, although the chance is rather slim. At almost all point shows, WD usually takes home not only his ribbons and points, but trophies and cash prizes as well.

    This leaves the WD as the only class dog remaining in contention. He and his handler retire to worry about the immediate future, and the judge repeats the five classes for bitches. The blue-ribbon winners meet in Winners Class, and one of them is named Winners Bitch (WB). The available championship points for bitches belong to her, and again, if they total less than the five maximum at any one show, she has a chance to win more.

Now both WD and WB go into the next competition where, together with the champions of record of their breed, they compete for Best of Breed (BOB) or Best of Variety (BOV). This judging forms the climax at the breed level. When it's over, only one dog of the breed or variety will remain in contention at the show, and have a shot at greater glory. And in addition to the honor, the winner also takes home the coveted purple-and-gold ribbon. Usually, and always at the larger point shows (over two thousand dogs), BOB and BOV also win trophies and cash donated by the show's sponsoring club and by breed lovers.

Then, if neither the WD or WB has won out over the champions for BOB, the judge selects one of them to be Best of Winners (BW). The honor is meaningless unless one has picked up fewer championship points than the other. In rough collies, for example, WD may have been worth three points, but WB only a single point. If the judge puts the bitch over the dog for BW, she exchanges her single point for the dog's three. And happily, he keeps his three points. Happily for his owner, that is.

Finally, the judge checks the sex of the BOB and looks around for the best dog of the opposite sex. His choice becomes Best of Opposite Sex (BOS), wins a nice green and white rosette, and makes at least one owner happy. Otherwise, a meaningless honor.

At small shows, it is not unusual for a class dog to go all the way to BOB or BOV. Thus, when WD or WB goes BOB, he or she is the best representative of the breed present and the BW award is automatic. This seldom happens at the big shows, or in the popular breeds, anyway. The great, established champions are present in huge numbers and the nonchampion class-dogs, who are still proving their worth, are usually outclassed.

So that's what happens at the breed level. Since there are always scores of breeds plus varieties of some breeds present, that level of judging consumes most of the hours and eliminates the greatest number of dogs at any all-breed point show.

THE GROUP LEVEL

Since some of the AKC recognized breeds are rare, they are seldom seen at point shows. At the biggest shows, there will be around ninety BOB and BOV dogs. As noted earlier, each of these dogs belongs to a particular group, and now they proceed to the second level—the well-organized elimination that makes up the group judging.

For example, the boxer BOB is assigned to the Working group, and there—if all the other working breeds are present—finds itself competing with thirty other winners. It is the solemn duty of the group judge to pick four winners, and to rate them from one to four. At this level, the competition is very tough, for many of the handlers are professionals, and they know all the tricks of the trade. Artful handling can make a good dog look like one of the greatest dogs on earth—for a few minutes, anyway.

The odd thing about group judging is that it terrifies so many amateur handlers. A strong amateur who has successfully handled a boxer to BOB will suddenly become a nervous wreck and run around the show grounds trying to find an unemployed professional to handle the dog in the group.

If owning a Best of Breed dog is an honor, then owning the first-place winner in the group is akin to being knighted by the Queen. The dog has eliminated all the other dogs in its group, and proceeds to the final level of elimination—the Best-in-Show ring.

BEST-IN-SHOW LEVEL

The highest honor a dog can win at a point show is Best in Show (BIS). To go BIS just once in its lifetime may not be the dream of every show dog, but it is the ultimate dream of every show dog owner. While nobody else can see it, the owner is convinced that he wears a halo. The real glory belongs to the dog, but it's easy for owners to forget that. And who can blame them?

So that's the story of any all-breed point show. From the beginning to the climax, it's all a matter of elimination. And it's almost, but not quite, the complete story of how a class dog can pick up championship points. Normally, the nonchamp does harvest all of his points at the breed level. Still, if he's an outstanding dog, he does have a chance to pick up points at the group level and perhaps at the BIS level. To qualify for that chance, he must win big at the start and go BOB.

In all truth, this kind of big winning doesn't happen very often. For one thing, class dogs in most breeds seldom go BOB. It happens more often in the less popular breeds, and it was really for their benefit that the point system above the breed level was

Ch. Acadia Command Performance is being carefully posed. He was named Best in Show at the Westminster Kennel Club Show in February 1975. Three thousand twenty-eight other dogs were competing for the honor.

established. It's tough to win at the higher levels, but it's not an impossible dream, and here's how it did happen to a little four-pound puppy owned and handled by my good friend the late Aennchen Antonelli, who bred and handled some of the best Maltese in the world.

The Maltese is one of the toy breeds and usually ranks around fortieth in popularity. At all but the big point shows, the breed competition is usually pretty slim, so championship points are difficult to find at the breed level.

Sitar Dancer didn't discover this until she was eleven months old. The pup had ten points to her credit, including a major win of three points, and all won at big shows. She lacked five points and a major win when she arrived at an average-sized show of about twelve hundred dogs.

A few other Maltese had been entered in the classes, but they were absent. Since the puppy bitch Sitar was the only class dog present, she went WB and (later) BW automatically, but the wins meant ribbons, not points. There were two Maltese champions present. Sitar defeated them for BOB, but she still hadn't won any points.

As BOB, Sitar proceeded to the group level. There, to the amazement of the spectators and her owner-handler, Sitar won first place. Now, since she had defeated the best of the other toy breeds, she was entitled to the most points won by any toy breed at the show. Since BW in toy poodles had picked up four points, Sitar went from zero points to four points.

The winner of the Toy group went into the BIS ring against the winners of the other five groups, all of them famous champions. You guessed it! Sitar went BIS! And in so doing, she was entitled to the most points won at any breed level that day. Since there had been five points in German shepherds, the tiny bitch claimed those. This was a major win, of course, and it gave her just enough points to make her a champion.

Although Sitar won her championship as a puppy, something that does happen often in the toy breed (they mature earlier), her record is overshadowed by that of her own dam, Ch. Aennchen's Smart Dancer. That bitch won all of her championship points at the group and BIS levels. She, too, was amateur-handled by her owner all the way.

PREPARING FOR THE BREED RING

In one respect, dog shows have changed rather drastically over the years. The days of the great kennels are in the past, and the average exhibitors of today own just one or two dogs and handle their canine charges themselves. No matter their degree of expertness, the owner-handlers are known in the dog game as amateur handlers. That's you.

And then there are the professional handlers—fourteen hundred or more ladies and gentlemen who are licensed by the AKC and earn their bread by training and handling dogs owned by others. The latter are dog fanciers who hire the professionals for a variety of reasons: they are physically incapable of handling a dog, they don't have the time, they are too shy to perform in front of spectators, their primary interest is in seeing their names in the papers as owners of winning dogs, they are convinced that only a dog handled by a professional can win big (an odd view that casts shadows on the honesty of breed judges), or they just become too nervous when the chips are down. Although wealth helps, one doesn't have to be wealthy to hire a professional; those who do miss out on a lot of fun, thrills, and personal satisfaction.

Thus, the dog game continues on its merry way as the only remaining sport wherein amateurs and professionals compete at the same level. In football, for example, high school teams do not compete with the Green Bay Packers.

Competition is fierce at the yearly Westminster Show. Here the working group is being gaited before the judges.

The hallmark of an amateur handler is nervousness. Some amateurs get over this, but most do not. Some of my own friends have been handling dogs for twenty and thirty years, they are professionals in every sense but name, and they still become nervous as soon as they step into the ring. A case of personal jitters does not help your dog, of course. There are two well-known antidotes for nerves: realize that losing does not mean the end of the world, and learn to control your nervous system by attending a few match shows. Since the entry fee at a match show is usually a dollar, it's the economical way to learn. The entry fee per dog at a point show usually runs eight dollars, and more at the big shows. In the breed ring, the less jittery you are, the better your dog will perform. Tenseness does seem to run down a leash.

Since all a dog has to do in the show ring is wear a collar and leash as it stands at attention or gaits, there's nothing complicated about handling the dog. All that is really required for success is teamwork between handler and dog. The two must work as one and, ideally, unobtrusively. This is achieved by practice at home and at match shows.

The achievement can be time-consuming, but it should never be a problem. Assuming that man's intelligence fits into a shoe box, canine intelligence fits into a small matchbox. Anyone who can read and write and is not physically handicapped should be able to train the average dog. Every so often, of course, an extremely stupid dog comes along. It is trainable, too, but its intelligent owner must be more patient.

Since every show dog begins its career in the classes at breed ring level, let's take a look at what happens in that ring.

The breed judges are always the boss. By word or signal, they give the directions, and their decisions are final. Since they are concentrating on the dogs, they do not engage in long conversations with the handler, so one does not ask them about the weather or how their children are doing at college. Words are exchanged only if the judge asks a question, and the question is always related to the dog. Thus, when a judge asks, "How old?," it is improper to say, "Ten, but I will be eleven next month." Instead, give the age of your dog, in years or months. If you cannot remember precisely, guess and respond with something like "About fifteen months."

GAITING PATTERNS

The dogs are always gaited in the ring, either as a group, individually, or in pairs. Gaiting is just a show term for heeling; usually, a dog stays at its handler's left side and moves at a natural trot. Since the judge is studying the dog's movement, the first trick is to keep the beast from pacing (front and rear leg on one side moving in unison), an unnatural motion for every breed but one. The exception is the Old English sheepdog, whose breed standard permits "a characteristic ambling or pacing movement."

As the dog moves along at a natural trot, the handler travels at the same speed, and the total effect is togetherness. In the case of a toy breed, of course, the little pooch trots as the handler walks.

The biggest trick of all—and the one many amateur handlers fail to observe—is keeping the dog in full view of the judge. Judges are not blessed with superior powers of vision and cannot see through the human body. As several of the following diagrams reveal, the handler must sometimes switch a dog from left side to right side in order not to block the judge's view of the dog.

There's no need to diagram general gaiting. All of the dogs in a given class participate by gaiting in a line. The judge stands in the center of the ring as the dogs gait in a counter-clockwise circle. Since each handler has the dog on his left side, the judge gets a clear view of each dog.

After the dogs have been gaited in unison, they are usually stacked in a line and the judge goes over each dog to determine virtues and faults as specified in the breed standard. Next, each dog is gaited individually. Again, the judge is studying movement, and this time he's either refreshing his mind or double-checking on his first impressions. In the breed ring (and Junior Showmanship), judges stick pretty close to the traditional gaiting patterns.

Diagrams A and B show the simplest solo gaiting patterns. In both, X marks the spot where the judge stands, the solid line represents handler and dog, and the dog is on the handler's left side. In the case of an overweight handler, the judge's view might be blocked on a turn, but only for an unimportant instant.

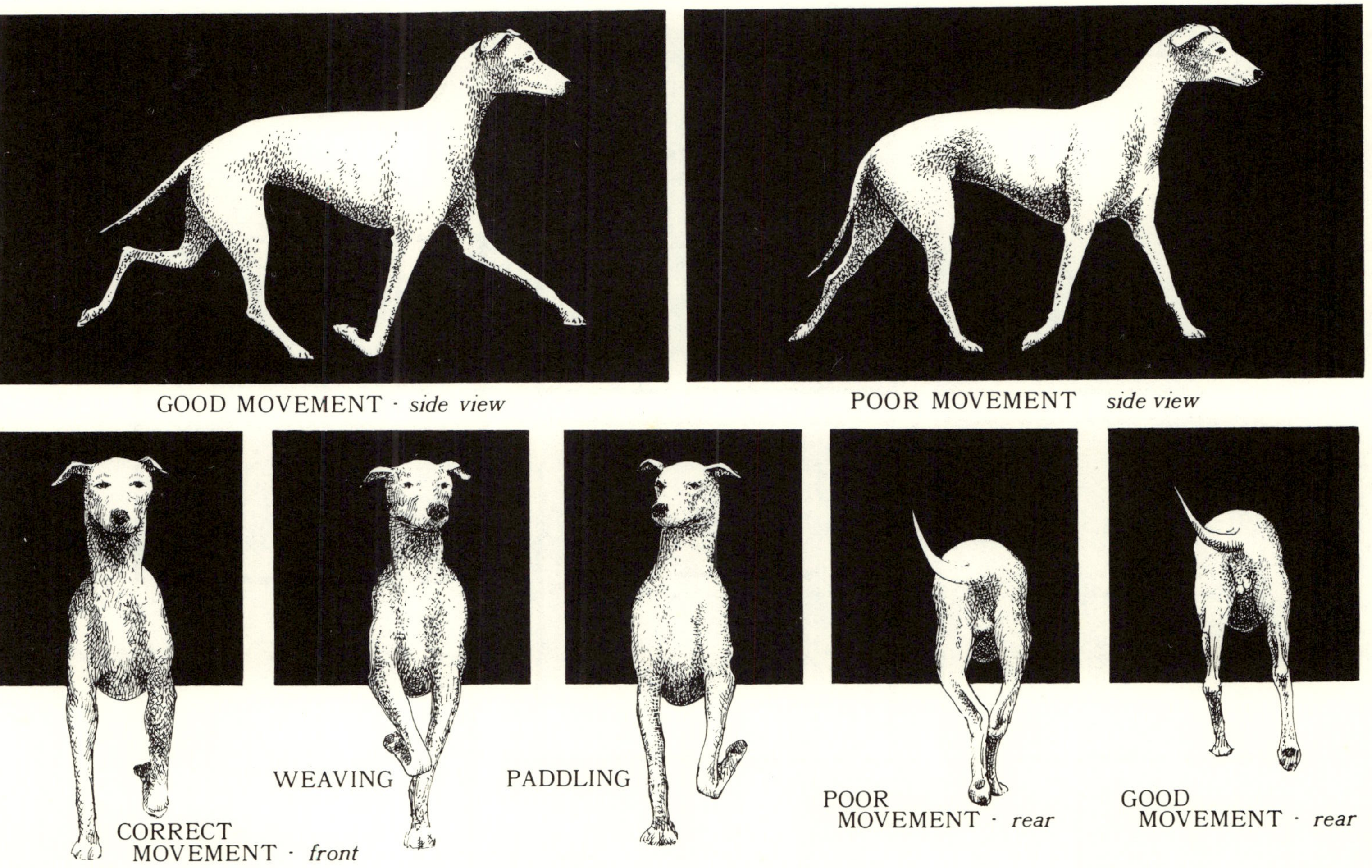

GOOD MOVEMENT · *side view*

POOR MOVEMENT *side view*

CORRECT MOVEMENT · *front*

WEAVING

PADDLING

POOR MOVEMENT · *rear*

GOOD MOVEMENT · *rear*

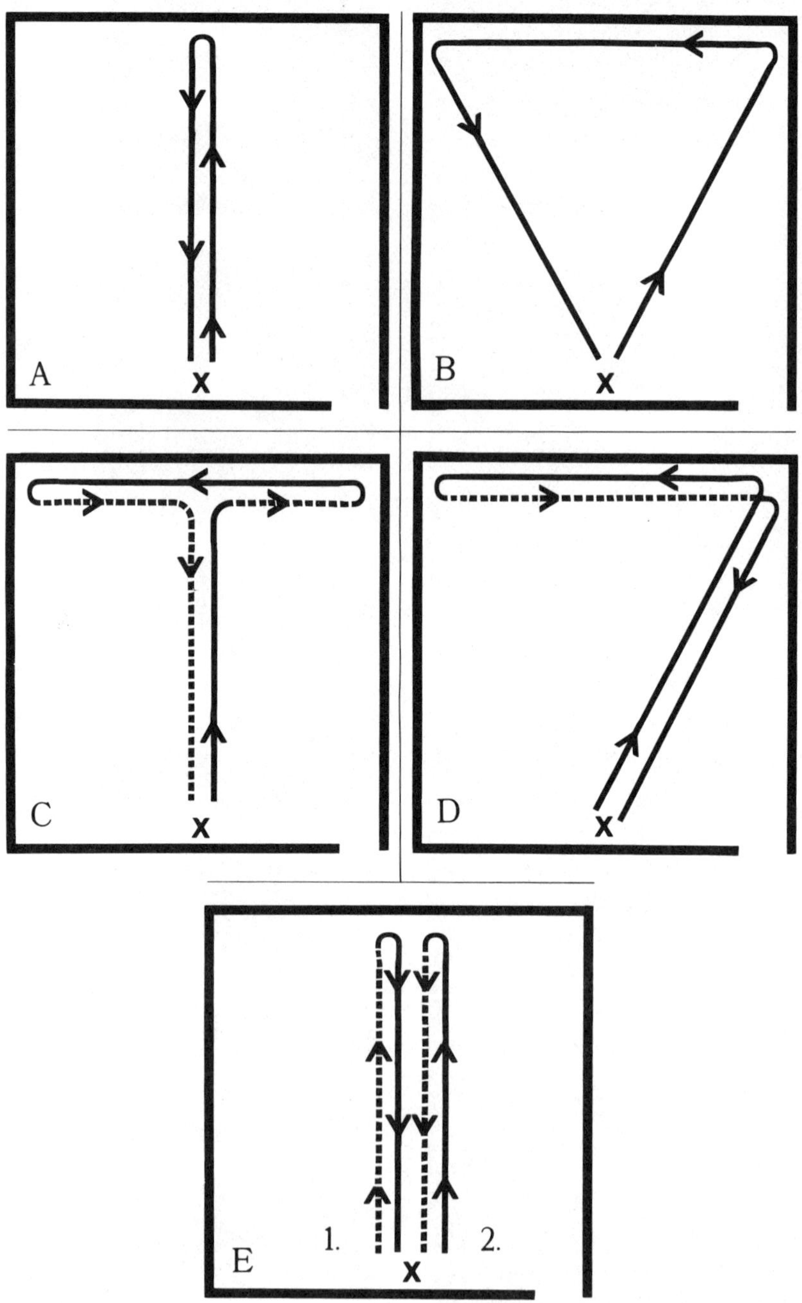

A
X
B
X
C
X
D
X
E
1.
2.
X

Every so often, a judge calls for a more complex gaiting pattern, or one that requires a shift of the dog from the left side to the right side of the handler. Without that shift, the judge gets a nice view of the handler, but he prefers to see the dog. When necessary, the change occurs on turns, with the handler switching the leash from one hand to the other and sometimes doing a little fancy stepping. Stumbling over one's dog does not help its chances, so wise handlers accustom themselves and their dogs to the change of sides while gaiting—and before heading for the point shows. In diagrams C and D, the solid line represents the dog on handler's left, and the dotted line means that the dog is on the handler's right. Again, the switch takes place on the turns.

Diagram E shows the gaiting pattern required by judges who can't make up their minds between two dogs. They want to give the win to the best mover, so they ask the two handlers to gait their dogs side by side. Going out, No. 2 dog is on the handler's left (solid line), while No. 1 dog is on the handler's right (dotted line). On the return, the reverse is true. All the way (going out and returning), the handlers keep their dogs reasonably close to each other, or no more than twelve inches apart. The diagram can't show this, but please believe it.

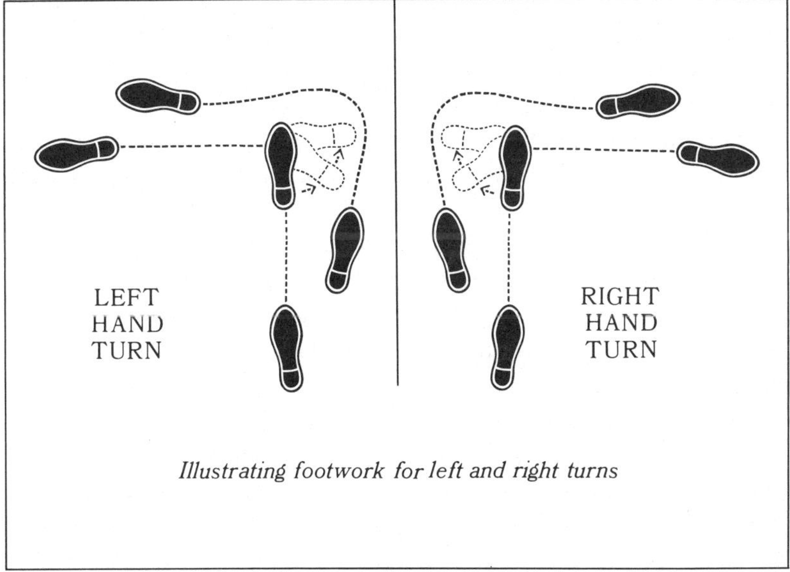

Illustrating footwork for left and right turns

TRAINING THE DOG

Training for the show ring can start at any age, or just as soon as a dog is accustomed to wearing a collar and doesn't fight a leash. Usually, a pup learns more quickly than an adult.

While any leash will do, I use a plain canvas-web work lead. It's cheap, durable, and washable. The best collar choices are a lightweight French choke or a nylon slip. A tug on the leash tightens either collar, doesn't hurt the pup, and teaches it not to stray from your side. A big, thick, heavy collar is useless and a pain in the neck to a dog.

GAITING. Gaiting amounts to heeling at a trot. Here's how to train a pup or a dog: Whether you are left- or right-handed, hold the end of the leash in your right hand. Extend the leash across the front of your body to your left hand, and then down to the dog's collar. Obviously, the dog is standing at your left side.

Note the proper way to teach a dog anything. First, speak his name. This attracts his attention. Then, after a very brief pause, give the command word: "Rex. . . . Heel!" The tone of voice should be normal and reasonably firm. Canine hearing is vastly superior to man's. Shouting is unnecessary, and it also irritates judges. Despite the opinions of many dog fanciers, judges are human. Fu Manchu says, "Judge who dislikes handler may dislike handler's dog. Explanation: Occidental human nature."

On the command word "Heel!", step off on your left foot. The motion of your left leg, the leg next to the dog, is a signal that you're going somewhere.

Your left hand is your control point. Use it to tug on the leash whenever the canine student lags, stops, or bounces ahead. The dog must trot along at your left side, and before long will realize that by staying there, it won't feel the irritating pull on the collar.

There's just no way of estimating how long it will take an individual pup or adult dog to learn how to heel properly. But pups under six months will usually agree to a couple of five-minute sessions a day; from six months to a year, they'll take fifteen-minute sessions before becoming bored; over a year, they can be worked a good twenty minutes before they become stubborn.

Obviously, the size of a dog dictates the speed of the handler. Toy poodles trot as their handlers take slow steps, but German shepherds trot naturally only when their handlers move at a fast clip.

Ideally, dogs always hold their heads up in the show ring. But while they may do this all the time during practice sessions, they must be watched in the ring. There, indoors and outdoors, other dogs have crossed the same surface, and they may consider their scents worth sniffing. A tug up on the leash will remind a dog to hold its head up. If the tug is accompanied by the quiet command, "Head up!", the dog will, in due course, bring its head up on the command, and the tug will not be needed.

In the ring, the leash is held in one hand only (the left), with the excess length gathered in your palm. Judges who know their job always ask for a loose lead. This means that the handler holds the lead (leash) in a slack manner, so that the dog is obviously holding up its own head without assistance. The reverse, or a tight lead, is called *stringing up*. On this taut lead, the dog must hold its head on high as it trots along. Professionals often string up their dogs to hide loose shoulders and imperfect elbows. On a loose lead, those dogs would collapse up front and appear to be floundering. Judges are seldom fooled.

STANDING. So much for gaiting, one of two things the show dog must perform in reasonable manner if it is going to impress a judge. Number two? Silly as it may sound, the dog must know how to stand. Stand properly, that is. "Rex. . . . Stand!"

With some exceptions, the proper show stance for all breeds is identical.

1. Up front, the dog (a) holds its head up and (b) its forelegs drop straight to the ground. The elbows are straight, too; the feet point straight ahead; and the legs are chest width apart. From any angle, the legs and elbows appear to hang straight from the body.
2. Topline (back) is level.
3. Aft, the dog's hindlegs are planted a bit wider than up front, with hocks straight to the ground. Angulation (curvature) from hock (ankle) to stifle (knee) to body is required in many breeds and specified in their breed standards.

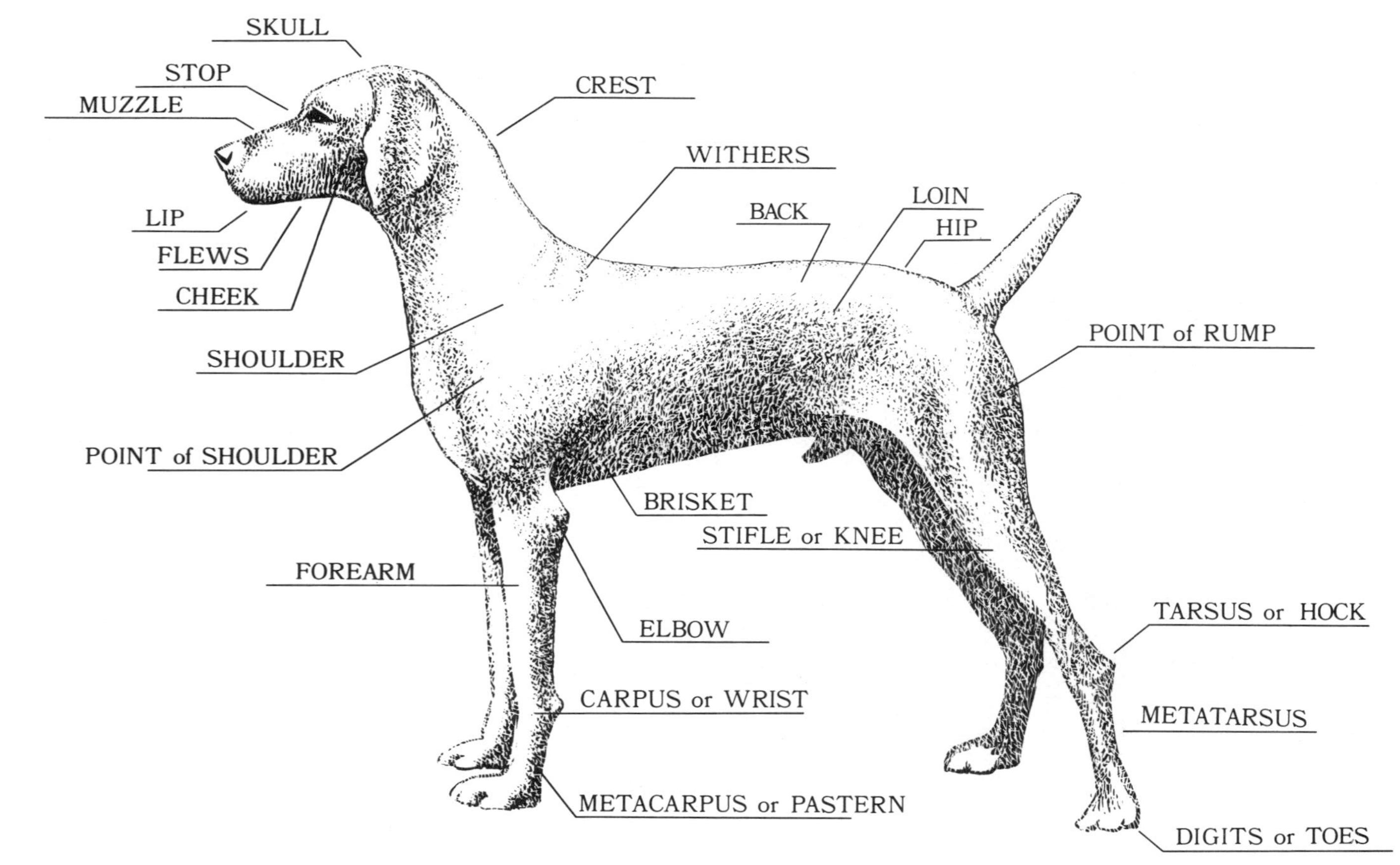
SKULL
STOP
MUZZLE
LIP
FLEWS
CHEEK
SHOULDER
POINT of SHOULDER
FOREARM
CREST
WITHERS
BACK
LOIN
HIP
POINT of RUMP
BRISKET
STIFLE or KNEE
ELBOW
CARPUS or WRIST
METACARPUS or PASTERN
TARSUS or HOCK
METATARSUS
DIGITS or TOES

The dog that stands correctly is the living picture of its breed standard, shows itself to the best advantage when viewed from front, side, or rear, and thus has the best chance of impressing judges. Indeed, some judges in the dog game are famous for selecting dogs that stand well, and present a pretty picture, over dogs that are obviously sounder in body and superior movers. Those judges, of course, started off by being in the wrong place at the right time. Fate had bathing beauty contests in mind for them.

The three specifications mentioned previously (up front, topline, and aft) hold true for all but a few breeds. Here's a sampler of some exceptions:

1. Bulldog. Forelegs have bowed outline; slight rise in topline from withers to loin.
2. Basset hound. Feet point outward, rather than straight ahead.
3. Bedlington terrier. Arched topline over loin.
4. English, Irish, and Gordon setters. Topline slopes slightly (down) from withers to loin.
5. German shepherd. Topline slopes slightly down, but a little more so than for the setters. Aft: one leg forward as if in semicrouch.
6. Pekingese. Toes point out (Charlie Chaplin style).
7. Welsh corgi. Forelegs slightly bowed and more so below carpus (wrist).

If you don't own one of these breeds, don't worry about the idiosyncracies. In any case, no matter what your breed, study the breed standard and good photographs, and don't be afraid to ask questions of any breed fanciers you happen to meet at the shows. For the AKC book of breed standards, see chapter 10. Your local library probably has it.

If a dog is untrained, chances are it will not stand correctly, or as we think it should stand. Just as too many people devote their lives to slouching and developing round shoulders, most dogs are willing to stand in the position they find most comfortable, and usually it's a pretty sloppy stance. Very few dogs stand correctly of their own volition.

Still, there's no need for owners to bang their heads against a wall. It is not difficult to train a dog to stand correctly. In my experience, the earlier one starts the training, the less time-consuming it

The bulldog (left) was bred from a long line of fighting ancestors.

The German shepherd dog (above) is loyal and courageous, with a natural aptitude for learning.

is for the trainer. And in keeping with the times, I call my training system the *space method,* since the pup or dog is trained above ground or floor level.

The space method does not require a collar or leash, but it does call for a platform of some kind. The platform can be a table, bench, box, or crate. It must be firm, so that the canine student will not become apprehensive. The surface is even, but not polished. The canine student must be able to stand without fear of slipping. A hard rubber mat can always be placed over a polished surface.

My own work platforms happen to be a redwood picnic table (outdoors) and a metal dog crate (indoors). On top of either, the student is about thirty inches up in the air. Even young pups will sense that they had better not jump from that height.

Now, my breed is the Labrador retriever. Adults run about seventy pounds. I am not a strong man, so I prefer to start training pups when they are about ten weeks old. Around here, a ten-week-old pup knows its own name, so I keep repeating its name and the verbal command when I work with it. The daily sessions are short—no more than three or four minutes—and within a week the pups learn how to stand pretty well. A few seconds at a time, anyway. Anyone will go crazy trying to make healthy, happy pups stand absolutely still in perfect position for a minute or longer.

I start by planting the pups' rear feet at the very edge of the platform. It doesn't take them long to sense that they'll fall into space if they move backward, so they don't. Then I plant one hand behind their rump, so that they can't fall, and the other hand under their chest. I lift them about three inches up front, and drop them. Usually, their legs and feet come down just right. If not, I correct the position of either or both legs by lifting at the elbow and positioning.

At this stage, I don't worry about how they're holding their head. Usually, it's all over the place, as their tongue tries to make contact with my face or hands. The trick is double-edged: keep them happy and don't let them know they're learning something.

After they're standing reasonably well on their forelegs, I correct their hind legs. They may need more spread, or one or both hocks may need straightening. Corrections are accomplished by lifting either leg at the hock.

The space method continues for about two weeks. At the end, the daily sessions are about six minutes long. If I keep talking to them—and I do—the pups will stand correctly for about thirty seconds. The talk consists of repeating the command when they look like they're about to move, and reassuring them that they're the best pups ever whelped. When any training session is over, the pup gets a tidbit and I play with it for a while.

Have the pups really learned anything? Not in the way we understand the term, but unless they are complete idiots they will feel better when they're standing the right way. Nature designed both man and canine to stand in a certain way. When you stand in balance, you feel better. So does a dog.

The only alternative to the space method, of course, is the traditional ground (floor) method. But on the ground, the pups have more room for action, and it's best to use collar and leash. My own system is to use the space method for several weeks, then continue the training at ground level with the pups on leash.

I walk the pups around, bring them to a halt, and hope for the best. If they have their limbs planted in the correct manner, they get praise and a tidbit. Otherwise, a tug on the leash might correct them; or bringing them forward a step or two may do the trick.

Does this sound like a great deal of trouble? You'll be happy to know that the daily sessions don't last forever. After the first month, two or three short sessions a week will suffice. There's no sense trying to pressure the pups into learning anything, and they can't be shown until they're six months old, anyway. So there's plenty of time, and when they do go to the show, they'll probably hold a canine West Point posture for a few minutes at a time. Few judges ask for more.

But which comes first? Training the dog to gait, or training it to stand? Veteran dog fanciers are divided on this question, and all sorts of nutty theories are heard when they talk about dogs.

It doesn't really matter. The only thing to remember is that both should not be taught at the same time. The smartest-looking pups or adults are not nearly as intelligent as they seem. They're not difficult to confuse.

I've tried both ways, and I vote for teaching stance before gaiting. Since the training sessions can be held indoors, weather and season are unimportant. In the case of a pup, it can be taught at a very early age. Also, I'm establishing a close relationship with the pups, and in the long run that will mean better teamwork. And since I use the space method, they're not going to go berserk when the vet places them on a table, or when I start trimming their nails. The pups become accustomed to human hands, and later, when they're in the breed ring, they won't flinch or break when a stranger (the judge) runs hands over them. And for all I know, the fact that I don't let a pup fall into space may establish a sense of trust in the pup's small mind.

No matter which thing they teach first, most owners of toy breeds use the space method for training their charges to stand. In the breed ring, toys are placed on a table when the judge wants to examine them. So the little pooches are trained to stand above ground or floor level at an early age.

The same goes for most owners of long-coated breeds. While grooming their pups, they teach the pups to stand properly. Since the grooming distracts them, the pups learn how to stand without realizing it.

A dog doesn't have to be a canine genius to learn how to gait and stand properly. When it has them down pat, more or less, it's ready for the match shows, or—if you're a big dreamer—the point shows. Simple for the dog, but not quite as simple for the handler. No matter how much your dog loves you, it doesn't have the faintest idea of what's going on in the show ring, and it's up to you to present it at its very best. If you hope to be successful, some simple but related things about handling must be kept in mind.

DIRECTIONAL VISION. Impossible as it may seem, you must pay attention to both the judge and the dog—both at the same time, that is. If you concentrate entirely on your dog, you may miss a direction from the judge. Judges have their own pet ways of giving directions: verbally, hand signals, grunts and nods, or a combination of these. But each judge follows the same pattern with each dog, and it is possible to determine this pattern by observing how the judge directs other handlers and their dogs.

On the other hand, if you concentrate entirely on the judge, strange things may happen to your dog. Usually, this happens when you have your dog standing (*stacked*) properly and are waiting for the judge to examine it. The moment you take your eyes off the dog, it may curve its spine, move a leg, or shift its weight so that it is leaning forward or backward. The movements can be almost imperceptible. You are permitted to use your hands in the breed ring, so correct your dog the moment you notice something wrong with its stance.

CLEAR VIEW. The judge must always have a clear view of your dog, and only you can obstruct this view. So the dog must always be between you and the judge. You never know when the judge is going to glance your way.

This is very important when the dog is standing. When the judge examines the dog's head, you move to the dog's rear, and vice versa. When the judge is on one side of the dog, you move to the dog's other side. Never, never block the judge's view of your dog.

BAITING. Baiting is a legitimate little trick used by most handlers to keep their dogs alert and showing expression. When two dogs are equal in conformation and gait, the alert, spirited dog will always win over the calm or droopy one.

In the dog game, alertness is known as *canine expression,* and relates mostly to the dog's eyes and ears. Its eyes show keenness or interest, and its ears are at attention. Thus, it is quite proper, unless the judge directs otherwise, to bait one's dog, and this is done by a quick motion of the hand in front of the dog's muzzle. It helps enormously if the hand holds a piece of dried liver or kibble.

Plenty of practice at home is advised. The dog must stand motionless in the ring while it is being baited. If it hasn't had any experience, it may forget its manners and leap for the bait. This always brings laughter from the spectators, but it doesn't help the dog's chances.

Some judges like to do their own baiting by making peculiar noises. Such a judge usually crouches directly in front of a dog

and makes the noises. If the dog shows alertness, fine. If the dog jumps for the judge's nose, too bad. So it is always a good idea to practice noise baiting at home, too.

While there are no AKC rules for baiting, consideration for other contestants is obligatory. A few years ago, a certain lawyer started handling his Labrador retriever at Eastern shows. The man tricked his dog into a state of alertness by throwing a full key ring against the ground. Each time, several other Labs in the ring dove for the key ring. As retrievers, they reacted instinctively, and nobody could blame them. Of course, they weren't helping their own causes.

That foolish lawyer would still be disrupting proceedings if a judge hadn't directed him to stop creating a disturbance in the ring. When the lawyer started to argue his case, she dismissed him and his dog. Moral: Keep the baiting subtle and nobody will mind.

GROOMING. Grooming is an inescapable fact of life for show dogs. They must be presented in good coat and clean condition. Obviously, the smooth- and short-coated breeds are less trouble to groom than the wire- and long-coated breeds. If you don't have a book that covers grooming of your breed, check out the list in chapter 10.

SHOW LEAD. For all but the giant breeds (Irish wolfhound, Great Dane, etc.), the show lead (leash) is the best bet to use in the breed ring. It is really both a leash and a collar, in that there is an adjustable, slip collar on the canine end. It is lightweight, strong and pliable, usually costs under two dollars, comes in many colors, and can be found in most pet stores. It is ideal for showing a dog, since the excess length can be rolled into the palm of the left hand. (One hand—usually the left—is used to pilot a show dog.) Once your dog has learned its basic lessons, use this lead during practice sessions at home.

Remember to practice baiting at home before trying it in the ring.

Timing. Plan to arrive at the show at least a half hour before your breed is to be judged. Judging takes place as scheduled. There are no delays. After you have entered your dog at a point show, the judging schedule will be sent to you.

Show Entries. Entries are not made in advance at match shows. Just show up with your dog and pay the entry fee, usually a dollar or two per dog.

It's a different story for point shows. The entry fee per dog usually runs about eight dollars, and more at the biggest shows. Every point show has a closing date, and an entry must reach the appointed show superintendent by that announced date. It's simple enough to make out the standard entry form and mail it (with fee enclosed) to the show superintendent. Check chapter 8 for a sample form.

A week before the actual date of the show, you will receive in the mail three important pieces of paper: (1) a judging schedule, advising you of the exact time and ring for all the breeds, (2) a handler's ticket, providing you free entrance to the show grounds, and (3) your dog's entry certificate and number (as it will appear in the show catalog). Before you enter the breed ring with your dog, a steward will provide you with this number on an armband. The latter is worn on your left arm, so bring along an elastic band to make it stay there while you are handling.

Where do you find entry blanks for point shows? There will be no problem if you attend a few match shows. Or contact any member of the nearest kennel club. Or check the upcoming dog shows in dog magazines (see chapter 10) and write the show superintendents. And if you follow my advice and observe at least one point show before entering your dog at one, the show superintendent's booth will have entry forms for several future shows. Should you visit a point show as a spectator, by the way, leave your dog at home. Only entered dogs are permitted on the show grounds or in show buildings.

Once you have entered your dog in a few shows, you will start receiving notifications of upcoming shows through the mail. This notice is known as a *premium list* and it gives all the necessary information concerning a particular point show in your area: date of show, closing date for entries, trophies and prizes, and names of judges for the various breeds. It also includes several entry forms.

Now, all the above represents the advance thinking you must do before you and your dog arrive at a point show. Once you are there and in the breed ring, the chips are down and you must continue to think.

One of the great myths of our times is that show dogs are unhappy animals. The plain truth is that an unhappy dog is always listless and stubborn and doesn't stand a chance in the breed ring. Show dogs happen to be among the happiest and best cared for dogs in America. The show dogs I've known have always been happier than their handlers. So maybe there is such a thing as canine ego. The average show dog loves to strut its stuff.

Every registered purebred, of course, is not eligible for the breed ring. A spayed bitch, for example, is not eligible, no matter how fine a specimen of her breed she happens to be. But the spayed bitch and almost all of the other registered purebreds that do not qualify for the breed ring can be entered in the two other forms of competition at the shows: Junior Showmanship and Obedience.

Next, Junior Showmanship. It's the breed ring all over again, but with this big difference: you are more important than your dog.

JUNIOR SHOWMANSHIP: FOR YOUNG DOG LOVERS ONLY

The sport of Junior Showmanship is for young dog lovers only. In the beginning, 1929, it was known as Children's Handling (CH), and it was really conceived to give innocent spectators at dog shows some action that they could understand. Later, the original concept was forgotten and replaced by the belief that the sport had been sent from heaven to stimulate interest in the fine art of handling dogs and, thus, to train a new generation of dog fanciers for the breed ring.

Those were the days when children were supposed to be seen and not heard, and CH gave the serious-minded ones something to do when they accompanied their parents to a dog show. The sport was so informal that a child could go to a show, borrow a stranger's dog, and take the dog into the competition. In spite of millions of published words to the contrary, that should give you a pretty good idea about Junior Showmanship: it is not the most difficult sport in the dog game.

At best, CH was sputtering when the newly formed Professional Handlers Association got behind it in 1933. While it's hardly likely that the professionals believed in the heaven-sent theory or wanted to cut their own throats by developing future competitors, it's probably true that CH would have faded away without their continued support. Still, only a few shows featured CH prior to 1950, the year the sport was renamed as Junior Show-

Junior Showmanship finals,
at the Westminster
Kennel Club Show, 1975

manship (JS). After that, JS found a home at more and more shows, and at six hundred of them by 1968. It was popular, but rather confused, it was still informal, and the rules were general and varied from show to show. The dog fancy's deepest thinkers wanted the Professional Handlers Association to devise formal rules and regulations for JS, and to supervise the sport, but that didn't happen. "We are paid to handle dogs and not to train young dog lovers," one professional informed me.

In 1971, more than eight hundred point shows were featuring JS. The AKC stepped into the act with a firm set of rules and regulations. It took about four decades for it to happen, but now JS is standardized. No matter what the host show, the AKC laws hold true in all of our fifty states.

And just what is JS? In a sense, it is the breed ring all over again, except that people—not dogs—are judged. The quality of the dogs in the ring is unimportant. The judge looks for the best handlers present.

You may compete in JS if you are not younger than ten and not older than sixteen—from your tenth birthday to the day before your seventeenth.

There are usually four classes in JS, two in Novice and two in Open. To keep the competition in perspective, or more or less fair and square, the classes have their own age limitations. Thus, a ten-year-old handler does not compete with a handler who is almost seventeen and has years of handling experience behind him. Here's how the various classes break down:

The beginner in JS must always start in Novice: Novice Junior Class, "for boys and girls at least 10 and under 13 years of age on the day of the show"; or Novice Senior Class, for beginners "at least 13 and under 17 years of age. . . ."

A handler remains in either Novice class until he or she wins a first place in a class of at least five entries. Now the young handler can no longer compete in Novice and must compete in Open: either Open Junior Class or Open Senior Class, the age ranges being the same as in Novice. Eligibility for the Open classes is immediate: the Novice winner goes right into the proper Open class at the same show.

The winner or winners of the Open Class become eligible to compete in a final class of JS, the Best Junior Handler Class.

This class is limited to handlers who, prior to the closing of entries, have already won at least five Open classes in previous shows, including wins over a total of at least thirty-five other actual entries. You must qualify for this BJH Class each calendar year.

That's the way JS competition is handled at most shows. At a few small shows, however, a limited number of junior handlers may be on hand, and there's just one Novice class and one Open class. In such cases, the ages of the handlers run from ten through sixteen.

And at some of the biggest shows, the regular classes are divided by sex: classes for boys only, and an equal number of classes for girls only.

A Novice win serves only to qualify the junior handler for the Open competition. Only Open wins count in the record books, and the name of the game is to record at least five Open wins in one year. Five (as of 1975) is the magic number that qualifies a junior handler for the JS finals in New York City. The finals are staged each February during the course of the annual Westminster Kennel Club show, and the winner becomes America's champion junior handler.

The first Westminster winner was a teen-ager named Betty Clark. In retrospect, she may have set a precedent. Down through the years, the majority of the national JS champions have been girls. While every champion I've met has confessed to having had the jitters at the finals, the young ladies, during the action, have always appeared more poised than the young men. Maybe they realize that losing is not a disgrace, that there will always be another Westminster, and that winning does not guarantee a lifetime of happiness or straight A's back at school.

Achieving those five qualifying wins is not as easy as you may think. In an average year, some twenty thousand junior handlers compete at the point shows in JS, and only about seventy-five qualify for Westminster. Although junior handlers are about evenly divided as to sex, more girls than boys qualify for the finals. This may indicate that girls spend more time training their dogs at home. At any rate, there's no need for women's lib in JS. What's needed is men's lib.

Beyond the satisfaction of winning and the attendant publicity in the local press and the national canine journals, there are also material awards at every show. As in the breed ring, four places are awarded in each JS class, and different colored ribbons denote the placings: rose for first place, brown for second, light green for third, and gray for fourth.

Winning handlers never seem to discard their ribbons. Some paste them in scrapbooks along with press clippings, others display them over the mantel, and still others sew them on pillows. One of my daughters used them for bookmarks.

Almost always, the prizes that accompany the ribbons are more generous than those given in the breed ring. Trophies, books, show leads, wristwatches, and fountain pens are among the most frequent prizes.

A licensed breed judge, a licensed professional handler, or an AKC approved JS graduate (now too old to compete) always judges the JS classes. The procedure is precisely the same as in the breed ring, with these two, important exceptions: first, the handlers are being judged, not the dogs; and second, a variety of breeds, not a single breed, are in the ring at the same time.

Almost every purebred dog over the age of six months is eligible for JS, so long as it is owned or co-owned by the handler or by the handler's immediate family: father, mother, brother, sister, uncle, aunt, grandfather, or grandmother. Immediate family also includes such relations as a stepfather or a half-sister. Thus, while you may handle a friend's dog in some classes in the breed ring (if you do not accept pay), you cannot handle that dog in JS. Unless, of course, the friend is one of the relatives listed above.

Assuming your dog qualifies on the basis of ownership or co-ownership, it may be entered in JS competition as follows:

1. If the dog is entered for the breed ring at the show, it automatically qualifies for JS.
2. If the dog is eligible for breed ring competition, but not entered, it may be entered in JS alone.

Now, what about the dogs who do not meet their breed standards and are not eligible for the breed ring: the spayed bitch, the white German shepherd, the boxer with natural ears? There's a loophole for those dogs.

3. If the dog is entered at the show in Obedience, it automatically qualifies for JS. As we shall see, dogs not eligible for the breed ring are almost always eligible for Obedience (see chapter 6).

Since it's the handler, not the dog, who counts in JS, any one of the 129 AKC recognized and listed breeds is eligible for this competition. And there's no law that says you must handle the same dog at show after show after show. So, if there's more than one dog in your family, try your luck with each one.

Training dogs for JS is just the same as training them for the breed ring. They must know how to gait properly and stand correctly. Teamwork is really more important here than in the breed ring. The handlers who are not in control of their dogs at all times don't stand a chance of winning.

The judging is trickier here, too, in that the judge will often do the unexpected to test the handlers' alertness. In going over a dog, the judge may place one of the dog's legs out of position. The alert handler will immediately correct the dog's stance. Or, when gaiting a dog, the judge may change position, forcing the handler to gait the dog at his right side in order not to obstruct the judge's view. Every judge has a bag of such tricks, and uses them to tempt handlers into making mistakes. In a sense, the judge is always testing the handlers.

Unless one has gone under the same JS judges before, it's impossible to determine just what will influence them. Usually, it's best to play it safe and handle as competently as you can. On the other hand, some judges have been known to fall for overhandling, which amounts to employing such tricks as stroking a dog's back to focus attention on its beautiful topline or holding up a dog's tail to show the perfect set of that tail. Charming the judge with pleading eyes and a big smile never seems to work.

The older the breed judges, the more they've been around, and the more likely they are to overlook the JS handlers who employ tricks and charm. They've seen too many adult handlers in the breed ring trying to pull the wool over their eyes. Overhandling under JS judges who are professional handlers never works. The professionals know all the tricks, and they won't be impressed by them.

If you are good at studying facial expressions, it will be to your advantage not to enter the JS ring first with your dog. When the dogs are called to be stacked, you'll be able to study the judge's reactions to the way a few other junior handlers are displaying their talents before the judge comes to you. Adjust accordingly.

One of the cardinal rules of JS is that the hotheads always lose. So if you're one of those, either stay at home or learn to control your quick temper. In the ring, when their dogs make even slight mistakes, hotheads react by using severe methods to make corrections. That's not kindness to animals, nor is it the way to a judge's heart.

Judges do have hearts. During one long, hot summer, I watched a ten-year-old boy do something that earned him JS wins at show after show. I wouldn't say he was the best handler around, but he impressed the judges by showing concern for his small dog, a beagle. Whenever possible, the boy stood between the broiling hot sun and his dog, thus providing shade for his dog. At times, of course, this blocked the judge's view of the dog, something a handler should never do. However, compassion for his dog was more important than polished handling in the eyes of certain judges, proving that sometimes following accepted rules doesn't really matter. Of course, if the youthful handler had made a big deal out of consideration for his dog, the judges would have seen through his act and withheld the wins.

While success in JS competition is never accidental, it's not very difficult to achieve. All it requires is a dog, daily training, and a smattering of common sense.

Ten minutes is about the average for daily training. Some dogs take less, some more, but all require less time with each passing week. The dog must learn to gait correctly on both your right and left sides; you must learn to use the leash in either hand, and both of you must learn to move along as one and at the proper speed, namely, the dog's normal gait.

When the dog is not standing correctly, you must learn to correct it instantly and deftly. Books cannot teach you how to do this. Experience will.

As for the common sense department, you'll win sooner if you keep some pointers in mind.

Grooming. Keep your dog's coat proper and clean. And dress neatly and comfortably yourself; in other words, don't dress as if you're going to the dogs.

Attention. Since JS judges are always looking for handling mistakes, more attention must be paid to them here than in the breed ring. Thus, always be sure, even when the judge is busy elsewhere, that there will be a clear view of your dog should the judge happen to glance your way. They always do. And often, when you are gaiting your dog, the judge will move to another place, so that you must switch the lead from your left to right hand. Be sure you have this maneuver down pat. It will come in handy.

Here are some other important things to remember when you take a dog into a JS ring:

Courtesy. Be courteous to the judge, and to your fellow handlers. For heaven's sake, never crowd another handler and his or her dog, and never laugh at another handler's mistakes.

Personality. Be yourself. Pleading eyes and fetching smiles do not impress a judge. Nor does gum chewing.

Sportsmanship. When you lose—and everybody does—a smile is worth a thousand tears. There's always a next time. Smile, thank the judge, and congratulate the winner. Losing really isn't the end of the world. And win or lose, keep your thoughts about other handlers strictly private. Word does get around about the complainers, and judges have ears.

The Eager Beavers. It would be very nice if all junior handlers were good sports, but human nature is a funny thing, and some junior handlers define sportsmanship as doing everything possible to make the other handlers look bad.

If you are handling a small or medium-sized dog, try to get behind the junior with the big Great Dane. If that handler is an eager beaver, he or she will try to overrun you when all the dogs are gaiting, and try to crowd you when the dogs are standing in line. Fortunately, the eager beavers are in the minority, but there's usually at least one in every JS class. Try to spot them and stay clear of them.

GROUND WATCHING. This applies to outdoor shows. Don't assume that all ground is always level when stacking your dog. If one foot is in a slight depression, the dog will appear off balance. So don't figure that you are glued to one spot. Move a few inches or feet until you find level ground, even if it means stacking your dog out of line. The judge will understand.

While there's no longer any need for the dog fancy to encourage new blood for the future, since there's barely room for interested adults anymore, JS continues on its merry way. Aside from its material rewards, JS is as good a place as any to start in the dog game, and a great place to pick up experience for the breed ring. Fortunately for those who are still shy of their tenth birthday, the minimum age is usually lowered to eight (and sometimes younger) at match shows, and almost every match features the sport. Again, the wins don't count in the record books, but neither do the exhibition games of professional football teams. The more you handle under JS rules at the match shows, the better prepared you will be for the stiffer competition in JS at the point shows.

According to many of the sport's graduates, JS helps young dog lovers overcome whatever personality traits they want to overcome, such as shyness, nervousness, and impatience. And given half a chance, it teaches courtesy, sportsmanship, discipline, self-criticism, and a long list of other virtues believed to be necessary for the balanced, full life.

Unless you are generally regarded as a pain in the neck, JS is sure to be your proving ground for the making of new friends. In some parts of the country, interest in JS is extremely high. Close to a hundred junior handlers clubs now exist, and there will be more next year. The Junior Kennel Club of Tucson, Arizona, is America's oldest. Founded in 1934, the club's current membership includes grandchildren of the founders. To find out about the club nearest your home, write the Junior Showmanship editor of *Pure-Bred Dogs—American Kennel Gazette* (see chapter 10).

A first-place win in open class by twelve-year-old Donald Sturz, handling a golden retriever at the Saw Mill River Kennel Club

If you like to write and receive letters, the same editor can supply you with the names of willing pen pals in your breed. This service is designed to stimulate interest in JS and purebred dogs, not romance. Still, it could be a start. The rest is up to you.

Is the lack of a purebred dog the only thing holding you back from JS, club membership, and a pen pal? If you can promise a good home and care, and pledge that you'll become an active junior handler, that busy man at the magazine can sometimes find a gift pup for you. Here and there, breeders are anxious to make dogless young dog lovers happy. How's that for the ultimate editorial service?

Here are a few final words on JS. As in the breed ring, entries are required at point shows. Depending on the show, the cost per entry ranges from zero to a dollar or two to the same amount as a breed ring entry. Shows featuring JS include entry blanks in their premium lists.

If you're at home in the saddle, you might be wondering if the whole idea for JS was borrowed from the horse show world's Good Hands Class for children. In that competition, the horses are only important as mounts, and the young riders are judged on their overall performance: seat, hands, and management of horse. Well, if JS is a borrowed idea, nobody has confessed. It's possible that a few horses and dogs know.

Now, while many young dog lovers find JS or the breed ring or both completely satisfying, there are those who claim that both sports are no more than child's play compared with Obedience. I happen to agree with those dissenters. The Big O sport calls for real training ability and above average canine intelligence. If you don't believe that, read the next chapter several times.

6 OBEDIENCE: THE EDUCATED CANINE

The dog show world's youngest sport is Obedience. It's also the most trying, and is difficult enough to make handling in the breed ring or JS look like a picnic. Almost any purebred of the 129 AKC recognized and listed breeds is eligible for Obedience, granted that he or she is six months old. Unlike the dog that is going for its championship (chapter 3), the Obedience pooch doesn't have to meet the specifications of his breed standard, nor must he be whole. Thus, the poodle with an undocked tail, the Doberman with uncropped ears, the white German shepherd, the monorchid male and the spayed bitch, and all oversized and undersized dogs are deemed acceptable for Obedience.

Indeed, only totally deaf and blind dogs, as well as vicious and lame dogs, are not permitted to compete in the sport. One of my daughter Cary's dogs, Peanut, was amazingly successful in Obedience, despite an unfortunate accident that left the yellow Labrador bitch blind in one eye. Peanut's limited vision seemed to enhance her power of hearing, and judging from the way she took the Companion Dog Excellent (CDX) prizes, it did not lessen her depth perception.

This is one sport in which the physically handicapped can compete. If you are confined to a wheel chair or must use a cane or crutches, but you are able to move around the ring without human assistance, then you can handle your dog in Obedience. In

recent years, several blind people have trained and handled their guide dogs to top honors in the sport.

A handler's age is unimportant, so long as one can control one's dog. At Obedience trials, it is not unusual to see a seven-year-old child putting an adult Great Dane through its paces, or a senior citizen doing the same with a Shetland sheepdog pup.

And ownership is unimportant. While almost all of the handlers are owners or co-owners of their dogs, it is permissible to handle a dog owned by a friend, neighbor, or stranger, so long as the dog meets the eligibility requirements. So, if you don't own a purebred, find one, offer to train it, and hop into the dog game. The owner, of course, must make the entry.

In this country, Obedience really got under way in 1936, the year the AKC gave its blessing. The big idea behind it was twofold: first, to prove that canine champions had intelligence as well as proper conformation, or brains as well as beauty; and second, to provide the owners of average or subpar purebreds with the opportunity of doing something with their dogs in the dog game. Or, in the words of the AKC, "To demonstrate the usefulness of the purebred dog as a companion of man."

While the sport has been booming ever since its inception, the first part of the big idea has not. While the average dog fancier is anxious to produce a champion, only a minority of the champions go on to Obedience. It's as if the owners of champions are afraid to expose the limited intelligence of their beasts, or maybe those owners don't have much faith in their own brain power. This sport calls for plenty of training, patience, perfect teamwork, and concentration from both handler and dog. If you and your dog can succeed in Obedience, then you are one heck of a good trainer-handler and really belong in the dog game.

Compared to the breed ring, Obedience is truly an amateur sport. There are no real professionals, and the closest to that designation would be (1) the amateurs who have put many dogs through Obedience and are thus experts, (2) the licensed AKC

There are several jumping exercises your dog must complete in order to win the more advanced Obedience degrees.

Obedience judges who usually work for travel expenses, if any, and handle their own dogs in the sport when they are not judging, and (3) the teachers who hold Obedience training classes for owners and their dogs.

I like to think of Obedience as the canine equivalent of our own system of education. A dog can earn any one or all four degrees.

1. Companion Dog (CD), a high school diploma.
2. Companion Dog Excellent (CDX), a college degree.
3. Utility Dog (UD), a postgraduate degree.
4. Tracking Dog (TD), an FBI degree.

The dog that wins all four degrees becomes a Utility Dog Tracking (UDT). It has no more Obedience worlds to conquer and is one of the smartest dogs in America, even if it continues to chew on rugs at home.

The TD degree can be won at any time. The other three must be won in the order named, and each is more difficult than the previous one. But any dog capable of copping a CD has the brains to pick up a CDX and UD, too. Let's say that CD is just a step. Then CDX and UD are flights of stairs. A dog's capability, however, must be backed up by handler intelligence. Obedience looks easy. It's not. But if younger dog lovers than you have succeeded, why not you?

Let's put TD aside for a while and concentrate on the other degrees. In each, a dog shoots for a high, perfect score of 200. Very few dogs achieve that perfection. But if the dog can score 170 or better, and is not disqualified, then it earns a leg. Three such legs mean a degree.

To understand how a dog can earn 175 points and still be disqualified, here's a look at how the scoring goes in the Novice Class, where legs on the CD are won:

1. Heel on leash, 40 points.
2. Stand for examination, 30 points.
3. Heel free, 40 points.
4. Recall, 30 points.

During the above exercises, the dog and handler work solo in the ring. The only other person present is the eagle-eyed judge, who is always looking for a perfect performance, but seldom finds it. Either the dog goofs, or the handler gives too many commands. Only on the heel-free exercise are extra commands permitted, but the judge docks points for each extra. At stake are 140 points for the first four exercises. To stay in the running, the dog must score at least half the points allotted for each exercise. Thus, if a dog lags too much or doesn't stay at heel all the time during the heel-free (off lead) exercise, the judge could give it 15 points, or less than half of the available points. The dog has blown its chances for a leg, even if it's perfect in all the other exercises.

Now come the final two exercises. Both are done in a group. There can be as many as fifteen handlers and their dogs in the ring at the same time. The exercises call for canine patience and immobility.

5. Long sit (one minute), 30 points.
6. Long down (three minutes), 30 points.

To the unknowing, those exercises look very simple. Actually, both are toughies.

Consider the long-sit exercise. In unison, the handlers command their dogs to sit and stay in place, then march across the ring (thirty feet), and then turn and face their dogs. After one minute, the handlers return to their dogs, and the exercise is completed. Even dogs that sit in sloppy manner will get at least fifteen points and stay in the running. But the dog that decides to lie down or take a walk blows all thirty points and is disqualified.

Anyone capable of reading should be able to train a dog to remain in the sit position for five minutes, or at least more than one minute. But that is at home. In an Obedience trial, many temptations rear their ugly heads. One of the most common is for the dog to break away and join its handler, visit a child who is wandering by, or jump out of the ring and hunt for some fun. Obviously, sitting for one minute makes no sense to it and is boring.

If the dog that breaks happens to be sitting next to your dog, your beloved might decide to play with it. Or, if seven dogs break, your dog might get the idea that breaking is the proper thing to do. Add the usual dog show sounds (whistles, shouts, crying children, verbal commands from a nearby ring), and maybe you'll agree that if sitting for one minute in a strange environment is a test for a dog, then staying down for three minutes (long down) is a noble canine accomplishment.

More dogs disqualify themselves in the long sit and the long down than in any of the solo exercises. From any handler's point of view, the sit and the down are the heartbreakers. But there is an easy solution: train your dog with other dogs. While you can go it alone and succeed with your dog in Obedience, the road to success is always smoother and more direct if you sign up with an obedience training school.

These training schools are now abundant; there will be more tomorrow; and unless you live in complete isolation, there are several within easy driving distance of your home. They are designed both for people who just want to find out how to train their dogs, and for those others who want to go on to the Obedience trials. Courses run eight to ten weeks, one evening hour per week, and tuition (for handler and dog) runs up to a high of thirty dollars.

Those are the private schools. Many kennel clubs and obedience clubs also offer courses at lower rates. And then there are other obedience training programs offered by civic-minded organizations, 4-H Clubs, and adult education groups (nonadults also welcomed). Some are better than others, of course, but all attempt to help people to train their dogs, and all have many virtues if you plan to go for your dog's Obedience degrees. The biggest virtue is that your dog becomes accustomed to strangers and strange dogs. The other important virtue is that you can correct your dog when it goofs, something that's not allowed at the actual trials.

If the above sounds gung ho for obedience schools, we're on the same wavelength. I've done it both ways, training solo and in group (school) for Obedience, and I'm all for the group method.

Now, obedience school is not the whole story. What you learn there with your dog you must rehearse at home with it. Fifteen minutes every day is the very minimum. Too many people overlook this. The fact is that an hour a week over eight to ten weeks is not going to turn out a well-trained dog. You have to work at it every day.

Training begins with the basic commands. Once the dog has those down pat, it is taught to combine the commands. Those basic commands are six in number: heel, stand, sit, down, come, and stay.

Heeling has already been covered (chapter 3), but that was for the breed ring. In Obedience trials, the dog at heel must sit at heel every time its handler comes to a halt. Here's how to teach the sit command, "Rex. . . . Sit!":

Start with the dog on lead and standing at your left side in heel position. Hold lead tight (short length) in your right hand.

On the verbal command, tug up with the leash as you push down the dog's quarters with your left hand. Keep repeating. Sooner or later, your dog will sit on the command and without the tug and push.

Give the dog five-minute sessions for about three days so that it has the command set in its mind. During this period, correct it with your hands whenever it makes a sloppy sit. Your dog should sit squarely, or at attention: faced to the front, rear legs tucked under, forelegs straight to the ground. A sloppy sit will cost points in a trial. The dog should sit close to you, but not touching your left leg or leaning against it.

Now combine the heel and sit commands. Command your dog to heel, walk along, halt, command it to sit. Late in the training session, substitute the tug up on lead for the sit command every time you halt. After two days, the dog should sit whenever you halt without either the verbal command or the tug. During the CD heel-on-leash and heel-free exercises the dog must sit whenever you halt, and you cannot use either the tug or the command. Furthermore, on the heel-free exercise, the tug is an impossibility since the dog heels off lead.

Once the dog has this heeling and automatic sit under control, it's time for the stay command, "Rex. . . . Stay!"

In the upper strata of obedience training, there is a diversity of opinion about teaching this command. The majority opinion says that the dog's name should not be spoken, since it is the only command not calling for it to do something. According to this reasoning, when a dog hears its name, it anticipates doing something, whereas the stay command means that it should do nothing. Thus, the dog becomes confused when it hears its name.

I hold with the minority opinion and believe that the dog that becomes confused upon hearing its name is a pretty dumb dog. So I always use the dog's name, and none of my dogs have suffered confusion. Maybe they do anticipate something and then relax happily when they hear the next word. Use the name or don't use it—the choice is yours.

The simplest way to teach the command is to have the dog off lead, but wearing a collar. Command the dog to sit at heel position. Next, simultaneously (1) give the verbal command, (2) swing your left arm in a backward arc until the palm of your left hand comes close to the dog's nose, and (3) step forward, leading off on your right foot.

You must be very observant and keep your eyes on the dog. If it doesn't stay at sit, grab that collar and make it sit. Note that with this command you step off on your *right* foot. If you use your left foot, the movement of the leg will signal heeling to the dog, and it will move.

The important thing to remember about the stay command is not to expect too much. During the first few sessions, don't expect the dog to stay at sit for over thirty seconds, and don't wander more than ten feet from it. Increase time and distance until it will stay at sit while you stroll off fifty feet and return, and always be lavish with your praise.

By combining the sit and stay commands, you train the dog for its long-sit exercise in Novice (CD). For the long-down exercise, here's the best way to teach the down command, "Rex. . . . Down!":

Put the dog at sit. Face it and either crouch or get on your knees. On the verbal command, grasp and lift its forelegs. The dog will go down. Repeat until it gets the idea without being touched.

If that doesn't work after two five-minute sessions, put the dog on lead and at sit. Face it, with the lead forming a loop from its collar to your left hand. The bottom of the loop should be about two inches above ground level.

On the verbal command, raise your right arm as if stopping traffic and step on the loop with either foot. The dog will go down, and it will associate the action with your right arm. Later, all you'll have to do is raise your arm and the dog will go to the ground. With this method, be sure to use lavish praise. This method is not cruel, by the way, and it won't hurt the dog.

Once the dog has learned the command, combine it with the stay command.

One more command to go: "Rex. . . . Come!"

Off lead, the dog is commanded to sit and stay. March ahead ten feet, wheel, and face the dog. Give the verbal command. If the dog doesn't come, entice it to come by combining the command with some such antic as hand clapping, going to your knees, or running away. When the dog comes, praise it. Repeat until it comes on the verbal command alone.

There are dogs that just won't come. In that case, use a long lead (ten feet) or a long length of rope as a lead. If the dog doesn't budge on the verbal command, jerk on the lead. If it still won't budge, haul it to you, hand over hand. It will get the general idea.

Even if you are not headed for Obedience, your dog should know all the basic commands. Once it knows them, use the commands once in a while so that it will remember them. An obedient dog always makes the best pet.

The Open (CDX) and Utility (UD) trials are much more difficult for both handler and dog. They stump many an adult who finds the Novice (CD) trials a breeze. Still, I know a six-year-old girl who has already handled her collie to a CDX, and an eight-year-old boy with two UD golden retrievers to his credit. For where to find the AKC rules on the Open and Utility trials, check chapter 10.

Whereas an Obedience dog must win three qualifying legs to earn each of the degrees discussed thus far, it needs only one successful try to gain the Tracking Dog (TD) degree. A dog wins or loses. If it loses, it needs more training before having another go at the TD.

Since following the scent of a stranger is the whole trick, the tracking trials are never held at dog shows. They are held over virgin, rough terrain. Although a lead (not less than twenty feet long) is used, the handler cannot guide the dog or signal to the dog in any manner. In brief, the dog follows a stranger's tracks (less than two hours old), for a distance not less than 440 yards, then locates an article hidden by the stranger (wallet, glove, shoe) at the end of the trail. There's no time limit, but the dog must work (not loaf or stray) at all times. Two judges who know the course of the preset trail decide whether the dog has won or failed.

It's unusual when a pup under ten months of age wins his TD. Most of the successful candidates are about two years old and have had months of training. Everybody seems to have a different training method, but it should be obvious that a second person is required. This assistant plays a game of hide-and-seek with the dog. The assistant runs a short distance across a field and hides, and you release the dog where the tracks start. At first, the dog may have to be guided on leash, but once the dog grasps the idea, guiding will be unnecessary. Then the track becomes longer and more difficult, and the time between laying the track and starting the dog broadens. The more your dog uses its nose, of course, the more efficient a tracker it will be. If you think hounds make the best tracker, you're right. The tracking test for the TD and specifics pertaining to the three other degrees are fully detailed in the AKC booklet, *Obedience Regulations*. It's free! See chapter 10.

I've watched thousands of people, young and old, getting their feet wet in the Novice (CD) trials. About half of them fail to realize that they are not ready, nor are their dogs. Maybe the dogs were brilliant at obedience school and even more brilliant during training sessions at home, but a real trial is a whole new ball game. The first few times out, handlers are sure to be nervous, and that won't help their dogs. Nor will the new environment and its strange noises and scents help the dogs. For too many people, the first few trials are a waste of time and money, as well as being bitter disappointments.

The way to avoid all of that is to take it easy and acclimate both yourself and your dog at the match shows. The trials at the matches don't count, of course, but the exercises and conditions are precisely the same as at the formal trials, the ones that count. After your dog has scored 190 or better at a few match shows, it should be ready to have a go at the real thing.

Almost all of the all-breed and specialty point shows feature Obedience. In addition, numerous Obedience clubs hold formal trials of their own. So no matter where you live, you're near Obedience trials, indoors and out, in every season.

Unlike the breed ring, a dog does not compete against other dogs in an Obedience trial. It is simply proving itself.

And compared to the breed ring, the loot is plentiful. Usually there are awards for the ten highest-scoring dogs in a given trial. Trophies or cash and often both. Then, depending upon donors, there are additional awards for the highest-scoring dogs in specified breeds. The bigger the dog show, the more awards.

Entries are made in the same manner as breed ring entries. For many shows, entries are limited, so check the premium list. This is particularly true of indoor shows, because of limited space. When entries are limited, get your entry into the mail pronto, and well before the closing date. Otherwise, your money is sure to be returned, and your dog will miss a chance at a qualifying leg. And since you're only human, you'll be sure to suffer frustration. Wouldn't you know it? At the trial your dog is going to miss, he would have scored a perfect 200 and become the envy of thousands of other less brilliant dogs.

THE RIGHT BREED FOR YOU

Nine times out of ten, the nearest breeder will be happy to recommend his breed as the right one for you—and then proceed to sell you a pup. While that breeder might be the most honest person in town, the choice of breed should be yours, not the breeder's. Granted that you have willing parents, of course.

Most dog lovers do seem to be born with preferences for certain breeds. If that's the case with you, the application of a little common sense in regard to size and coat should help you reach a final decision.

When it comes to size, give the dog a break. The bigger dogs are as adults, the more room they'll need for comfort, the more hard exercise they'll need for good health, and the more unintentional damage they'll create. As for the coat, give yourself a break and put your life style first. Short and smooth coats require minimum grooming, and all the others are time-consuming. A light coat, of course, needs more care than a dark one.

Once you've selected your breed, there's always the matter of sex. Insofar as the dog show sports are concerned, the matter is unimportant, since the sexes have equal rights. This does not alter the fact that a bitch in season would create havoc at a show and should be left at home. She might have to skip a few shows now and then. However, that's not much of a disadvantage when you consider another fact: a bitch is usually easier to train than a male.

Here we are concerned with the best bets among the AKC breeds for the three sports of the dog show world. Hopefully, the insights that follow will help you determine your choice of breed.

BREED RING

Remember that only the registered breeds are eligible for championship points. A perfect border collie, then, cannot become a champion. So, if you have a championship in mind for your dog, it must belong to one of the 121 breeds that are fully recognized by the AKC.

It is a truism of the dog game that a good dog of any one of those breeds can become a champion as long as it is handled with some degree of finesse and shown often enough. Granted that its handling is adequate, a good dog can win its title in a minimum of three shows. There is no maximum number of shows. It can take ten shows, or it can take forever.

The breed ring is full of uncertainties: since judges are human and lack divine powers, they tend to interpret breed standards differently, and a dog that is rated by one judge as close to perfection ("Best beagle I've seen in fifty years") may not get a second look from another judge at a different show on the very next day ("Tail is too long").

And then there is the individual personality of show dogs. Basically, they must be happy, outgoing dogs, but they might not show at their best during a thunderstorm, or the noise and confusion of an indoor show might toss them for a loss. Even the best dogs have their odd, little traits. A friend of mine once owned a magnificent Afghan that hated to travel long distances. If the show was no more than fifty miles from home, the dog was usually a sure winner, but if the show was one hundred miles from home, the dog seemed to lose its spirit, drag itself around the ring, and lose. Like people, some dogs are oddballs.

Finally, the big hazard in the breed ring for the amateur handler is the professional handler. For a fee, the professional handles dogs for owners who have an intense desire to win. Since

Alaskan Malamutes

English setter puppies

American cocker spaniel

Yellow Labrador retriever

handling is their livelihood, they regard handling as a business and not a sport, and they are expert businessmen. Most pros know all there is to know about the dogs they're handling; each has a bag of tricks, and can make an average dog look like a world-beater for enough time to impress a judge. Quite often then, the best dog in the ring doesn't win, because its owner, an amateur handler, hasn't learned how properly to present it.

Fewer than fifteen hundred professionals are licensed by the AKC. Fortunately for the amateurs, all are never present at a given show. Those who are present will be handling from a few to a couple of dozen dogs in different breeds. While it is true that some amateur handlers defeat the professionals at any given show, the competition is more difficult for the amateur when a number of professionals are in the ring. Thus, the average amateur—young or adult—stands a better chance of success by avoiding the professionals. And since more dogs of the very popular breeds are shown, the top twenty breeds are the ones in which the professionals are the most abundant. In those breeds (see chapter 2), it's a little tougher and it takes longer for amateurs to win a championship title for their dogs. Not impossible, just tougher. If you can handle a poodle or a German shepherd to its championship within ten shows, you are a top handler and on a par with the best professionals.

While it may seem odd, the average young handler is often more successful than the average adult handler. Proper handling, or teamwork with one's dog, looks much simpler than it really is. Perhaps adults assume that what looks simple really is simple, and that hard training at home is both unnecessary and a bore. The thousands of youthful handlers who succeed with their dogs in the breed rings every year provide the proof that they think otherwise: training and patience do pay off.

So the best of luck, whether you intend to show one of the popular breeds or not. If your dog is a good one, sooner or later you can succeed with any breed.

JUNIOR SHOWMANSHIP

All the 121 recognized breeds and the 8 listed (miscellaneous) breeds are eligible, but it's the handling, not the breed, that matters. On the surface, then, any breed should do.

But unless you happen to be pint-sized, it always takes more handling skill to win with one of the very small breeds, such as any of the toys. This is especially true at outdoor shows, where the ground is seldom absolutely level, and the handler must be—among other things—extremely careful in stacking his dog. If a Chihuahua stands with its front feet in a slight depression, for example, its topline will appear to run uphill, whereas an even topline is desired. In the breed ring, the tiny breeds are stacked on a table, one by one, so that judges can study conformation without getting down on their hands and knees. But tables are not always provided in the JS ring.

And then there is the gaiting. At least once, all the dogs will be gaited together in a huge circle. If your dog is a tiny toy poodle and an Irish wolfhound is next in line, your dog just can't gait fast enough and is in danger of being trampled.

Thus, to enhance your own chances of winning, go to the medium-sized and big breeds. If you have a choice, that is.

OBEDIENCE

Again, all the breeds—registered and listed—are eligible. The records prove that all these breeds are capable of picking up the CD, CDX, and UD degrees.

It's the TD that causes trouble with a few breeds: those with pushed-in faces, such as the French bulldog and the pug. Obviously, they were not bred for scenting power, and they just don't have it.

Because of their keen noses, the hound and sporting and terrier breeds are the easiest to train for the TD. They are the best bets for that particular degree.

There's no need for second-guessing the best breeds for the other three degrees. The poodle, German shepherd dog, Shetland sheepdog, Doberman pinscher, collie, Great Dane, and all the sporting breeds are the proven stars of the Obedience sport. While this may or may not prove that these breeds are the most intelligent ones around, their owners think they are, and the breeds do seem to pick up the fine points of the sport with the greatest ease.

BEFORE THE SHOW

If you've read along this far, chances are that you and your purebred will give one or all three of the sports open to you in the dog game a try. So here's some valid advice that most veterans will approve. All of it is based on experience.

First, you must do some advance planning, so that—win or lose—you and your dog will have a great day at your first dog show and all the other shows in the future.

GETTING THERE. Study the road map so that you'll know the best route to the show. Estimate travel time from home to show, plus a half hour, just in case of unexpected delays: heavy traffic, detours, flat tires, or losing your way. Once you get within about a mile of the show site, watch for small signs that point to the show.

Thus, if it takes one hour to get from your home to the show, figure on an hour and a half. If your dog is due in the ring at 11:00 A.M., you should leave home not later than 9:30 A.M. Right?

In order to look its best in the ring, every dog needs a bath once in a while.

Wrong! Add one more hour and leave at 8:30 A.M. While this will get you to the show fifty or sixty minutes ahead of time, it gives you plenty of time for parking, a little grooming of the dog (if necessary), exercising it, and permitting it to answer nature's calls. As for the latter, breed ring and JS judges frown upon dogs that relieve themselves in the ring. In Obedience, the dog is disqualified.

Except for the big shows, most of the other shows, indoors and out, are now unbenched. This means that at most shows you will need a place to park your dog, and a dog crate is the answer to that. The right-sized crate is one that your dog can stand in without banging its head against the top.

If there's a station wagon in the family, solid metal and wooden crates are ideal. A dog is safest when traveling in a crate. Most just relax and sleep all the way to the show. Then there are folding, wire crates that can be placed in an auto trunk or strapped onto an auto top carrier. At all unbenched shows, areas are set aside for dog crates. At outdoor, unbenched shows, open-sided tents serve the same purpose, and also serve as protection against the sun's rays and rain. Very few dog shows are cancelled, by the way. They go on as scheduled, no matter the weather.

Okay. Let's assume you've arrived at the show grounds an hour ahead of time, all the little details have been covered, and you still have twenty minutes to kill before you and your dog are due in the ring. Fine, park your dog in the crate and take a fifteen-minute stroll. When you return, your dog will be happy to see you and on its toes, or in the right mood for strutting its stuff in the ring.

Many handlers like to arrive at a show a couple of hours early, so that they'll have plenty of time to give their dogs some extra training. While there's nothing wrong with this insofar as the breed ring and JS are concerned, it's wise to know one's dog. Like overtrained fighters, some dogs fail to do their best in the ring.

If the dog is headed for Obedience, forget about the last-minute training. If you're caught training your dog on the show grounds before it goes into the ring, the dog will be disqualified and you forfeit the entry money. That's the AKC law, and you'd better believe it.

FEEDING. A dog always performs best on an empty stomach. So even if you usually feed your dog in the morning, don't do so on a show day. A few licks of water will suffice prior to taking off for the show. Neglect that advice and you run the risk of car sickness, an accident in the ring, or a dull performance.

Now, this just isn't cruelty to animals. A dog can go for days without any nourishment—and for a much longer period with only water—and not suffer. Feed your dog after you return home from the show, and then go back to its customary dinner hour on the next day. If the dog is a pup and still on two meals a day, skip the first meal and make the second one a little bigger.

At the show, offer your dog a little water soon after you arrive, and again after it's through performing for the day. Obviously, since you'll need something to hold the water, it's wise to bring along a small pan or bowl. While fresh water is always available at dog shows, sometimes one must walk a country mile to find it. So I always bring a jug of water from home. When I forget, I buy milk at the refreshment stand. In hot weather, milk is a better choice.

Food should not affect your preformance as a handler, so have a hearty breakfast. It will help to calm your nerves.

EQUIPMENT. If you wait until the morning of a dog show to gather the necessities, you're almost sure to forget something that you're going to need at the show. The simple cure for forgetfulness is to make out a checklist, go over it the night before the show, collect all the items, and store said items in the car.

The checklist depends upon your dog's breed, of course. A poodle owner would not approve of mine, but a Labrador's requirements aren't many. For an outdoor show, here's my checklist:

1. Map.
2. Dog's entry ticket.
3. Water and dog's drinking pan.
4. Dog crate.
5. Two old towels, just in case of rain and mud. A dog should always be clean in the ring.
6. Hard-bristled dog brush for last-minute grooming, if necessary.

7. Work lead and show lead.
8. Food and drink for personal pleasures.
9. Extra money (stored in wallet) for anything I might want to buy at show: show catalog, new lead, books, magazines, novelties, etc.
10. Raincoat for myself, just in case.
11. Something for dog to chew (nylon bone or rawhide) in case it wants to amuse itself during trip.
12. Kibble or dried liver for baiting.
13. Lucky rabbit tail.

Of course, that last item may seem foolish, but it does give me moral support. When I forget to bring that lucky charm, my dogs never seem to win. Of course, they lose, too, when I bring the charm, but that's the dog game.

Whether you pack a lucky charm or not—and thousands of people do—the main thing is to bring along everything that you think you'll need for both your dog and yourself. If you gather everything and pack it away the night before the show, then all you have to think about is setting the alarm clock. Rise and shine when it sounds off the next morning. Dog shows do not wait for tardy dogs.

One more thing: decide what you're going to wear before you drop off to sleep. And a tip for young ladies: don't wear high heels. A dog show is not a fashion show, and high heels hinder rather than help a handler in the ring. Overall, dress in comfort, but don't dress like a bum.

Canine Health. If any dog needs booster shots, it's the one that goes to the dog shows. The big dangers are the infectious canine diseases: distemper, hepatitis, and leptospirosis. There are hundreds and sometimes thousands of dogs at a show, they come from far and near, and a few at any show are owned by careless people. Some of those owners are stupid, some negligent, some forgetful, and some blissfully unaware of the facts of life. The latter are well-meaning people who suddenly remember that their dogs need booster shots, rush their dogs to the vet, and then show those dogs the next day.

The important thing that they don't know is that the shots do not become effective and provide immunity for another fourteen days. If you are taking your dog to the shows, for heaven's sake keep the records of its shots up-to-date, and don't enter it at a show within two weeks after the most recent booster shot.

Now, just for emphasis, there's at least one veterinarian on duty at every dog show. They do not inspect every dog entered in the show, but just those brought to their attention for one reason or another. And even if they did inspect every dog present, they would have no way of suspecting or identifying the carriers—those dogs that carry and spread a disease, although they are not affected, and thus appear to be in the best of health. So, while every dog at a dog show is supposed to be healthy, some are not, and some that are can spread a disease. Don't gamble your dog's health. If you can afford to feed it and pay the show entries, then you can certainly afford the booster shot. In my neck of the woods, the vets charge about sixteen dollars for permanent shots (good for one year) and eight dollars for booster shots (good for another year). Where you live, it may cost a little less or a little more. Whatever the cost, it's worth it.

And then there is the matter of rabies. If a rabid dog bites your dog, there's no way you can save your dog. I have never heard of a rabid dog being present at a dog show, but I have witnessed dogs biting other dogs. This does not happen with frequency, but it does happen. A dog that bites, of course, is a vicious dog, and is not eligible for any of the dog show sports. Unfortunately, the AKC does not have a private force of investigators, so it's up to the owners to observe the rule and viciousness becomes a matter of personal interpretation. If they love their dog, the nicest people you know will not admit that their dog is vicious. "Nervous, maybe, but not vicious," they will say. "Anyway, every child he's bitten was teasing him. He was just protecting himself. Self-defense is not viciousness."

The plain truth that hardly anybody in the dog game wants to admit is that some dog fanciers do bring vicious dogs to the shows. All of the owners that I have known have been adults, highly regarded in their communities, and normal in all other respects. They just happen to be nutty when it comes to their dogs. "He didn't mean to bite, he was just playing a bit rough," is the commonest excuse.

So, at any dog show, it's best to stay alert and keep your dog away from any beast that looks or sounds vicious. Maybe it's not vicious, but why take a chance? While it's a pretty safe bet that the unfriendly beast is not rabid, don't back the bet with money.

You may live in a community where every licensed dog must have a rabies shot. If so, your dog is lucky, for it has immunity against such other rabid animals as stray dogs, foxes, and bats. Rabid cats are rare and getting rarer.

The rabies shot is not given before a pup is six months old. There are a couple of types of shots; the one I use on my dogs provides immunity for two years, then a booster shot provides immunity for another two years. Here, where the altitude is high but the income is average, the cost per shot is eight dollars.

ENTRY FORMS. While making out entries for dog shows is a simple matter, many entries are returned because they are made out incorrectly or incompletely. Unless your handwriting is very clear, it is always best to type out the entries.

The entry form for breed ring and Obedience is identical, but if you plan on entering your dog in both sports at the same show, then a single entry and fee is required for each sport.

The names on the breed ring entry shown here are for a mythical dog and owner (fig. 1). While the form has been completed and signed in proper manner, the owner reveals in the box headed Additional Classes that he is either new to the dog game or a foolish person. He is trying to make sure that his dog will win at least one class and thus be eligible for the Winners Dog competition. But if the dog is defeated in just one class, he will not be eligible for that competition, since the winning dog in that one class is obviously a superior dog. Entering a dog in more than one class is also expensive, since the entry fee is separate for each class. For this eight-dollar show, the owner handed over sixteen dollars.

The SIGNATURE line at the bottom is for the owner or co-owner of the dog: in your case, you or a member of your family. "Agent duly authorized" means a professional handler.

In the case of this entry, the owner's daughter has decided to enter JS with the same dog. For this particular show, another eight-dollar entry fee (fig. 2) is required for JS.

OFFICIAL AMERICAN KENNEL CLUB ENTRY FORM

FARMINGTON VALLEY KENNEL CLUB

July 6, 1974

Polo Frounds, Farmington, Conn.

All Breed & Obedience

(Unbenched)

Entry Fees: $8.00

I ENCLOSE $ 24.00 **for entry fees.**

● **IMPORTANT—Read Carefully Instructions on Reverse Side Before Filling Out**

Breed Airedale

Variety See Instruction #1, reverse side (if any)

Sex Male

DOG Show Class See Instruction #2, reverse side (Give age, color or weight if class divided) Open

Obedience Trial Class

If dog is entered for Best of Breed (Variety) Competition—see Instruction #3 reverse side **— CHECK THIS BOX** ☐

Additional Classes American-Bred

If entry of dog is to be made in Jr. Showmanship as well as in one of the above competitions, check this box, and fill in data on reverse side. [X]

If for Jr. Showmanship only then check THIS box, and fill in data on reverse side. ☐

Name of Actual Owner(s) See Instruction #4, reverse side John Wuzzle

Name of Licensed Handler (if any) [**handler**] ●

Full Name of Dog Beefeater Bingo ●

Insert one of the following:
AKC Reg. # R780125
AKC Litter #
I.L.P. #
Foreign Reg. # & Country

Date of Birth 6/5/73

Place of Birth [X] U.S.A. ☐ Canada ☐ Foreign ●
Do not print the above in catalog

Breeder, Peter Wolcott ●

Sire Ch. Smokey Joe

Dam Ch. Beefeater Molly ●

Owner's Name John Wuzzle
(Please print)

Owner's Address 506 Harmony Road

City East Harmony **State** Conn. **Zip Code** 06091

I CERTIFY that I am the actual owner of this dog, or that I am the duly authorized agent of the actual owner whose name I have entered above. In consideration of the acceptance of this entry, I (we) agree to abide by the rules and regulations of The American Kennel Club in effect at the time of this show or obediance trial, and by any additional rules and regulations appearing in the premium list for this show or obedience trial or both, and further agree to be bound by the "Agreement" printed on the reverse side of this entry form. I (we) certify and represent that the dog entered is not a hazard to persons or other dogs. This entry is submitted for acceptance on the foregoing representation and agreement.

SIGNATURE of owner or his agent duly authorized to make this entry ● John Wuzzle

FIGURE 1

OFFICIAL AMERICAN KENNEL CLUB ENTRY FORM

SPRINGFIELD KENNEL CLUB

May 10, 1975

Exposition Grounds, West Springfield, Mass.

All Breed & Obedience

(Unbenched)

Entry Fees: $8.00

I ENCLOSE $ 16.00 for entry fees.

• IMPORTANT—Read Carefully Instructions on Reverse Side Before Filling Out

Breed	Variety (if any) See Instruction #1, reverse side	Sex
Airedale		Male

DOG Show Class — See Instruction #2, reverse side (Give age, color or weight if class divided)	Obedience Trial Class
	Novice A
If dog is entered for Best of Breed (Variety) Competition—see Instruction #3 reverse side — CHECK THIS BOX ☐	Additional Classes

If entry of dog is to be made in Jr. Showmanship as well as in one of the above competitions, check this box, and fill in data on reverse side. [X]

If for Jr. Showmanship only then check THIS box, and fill in data on reverse side. ☐

Name of Actual Owner(s) — See Instruction #4, reverse side: John Wuzzle

Name of Licensed Handler (if any): [handler] •

Full Name of Dog: Ch. Beefeater Bingo •

Insert one of the following:
AKC Reg. # R780215
AKC Litter #
I.L.P. #
Foreign Reg. # & Country

Date of Birth: 6/5/73

Place of Birth: [X] U.S.A. ☐ Canada ☐ Foreign •
Do not print the above in catalog

Breeder, Peter Wolcott •

Sire: Ch. Smokey Joe

Dam: Ch. Beefeater Molly •

Owner's Name: John Wuzzle
(Please print)

Owner's Address: 506 Harmony Road

City: East Harmony State: Conn. Zip Code: 06091

I CERTIFY that I am the actual owner of this dog, or that I am the duly authorized agent of the actual owner whose name I have entered above. In consideration of the acceptance of this entry, I (we) agree to abide by the rules and regulations of The American Kennel Club in effect at the time of this show or obediance trial, and by any additional rules and regulations appearing in the premium list for this show or obedience trial or both, and further agree to be bound by the "Agreement" printed on the reverse side of this entry form. I (we) certify and represent that the dog entered is not a hazard to persons or other dogs. This entry is submitted for acceptance on the foregoing representation and agreement.

SIGNATURE of owner or his agent duly authorized to make this entry • John Wuzzle

FIGURE 2

Single copies of the latest editions of the "Rules Applying to Registration and Dog Shows" and "Obedience Regulations" may be obtained WITHOUT CHARGE from any Superintendent or from THE AMERICAN KENNEL CLUB, 51 MADISON AVENUE, NEW YORK, N. Y. 10010.

AGREEMENT

I (we) acknowledge that the "Rules Applying to Registration and Dog Shows" and, if this entry is for an obedience trial, the "Obedience Regulations," have been made available to me (us), and that I am (we are) familiar with their contents. I (we) agree that the club holding this show or obedience trial has the right to refuse this entry for cause which the club shall deem to be sufficient. In consideration of the acceptance of this entry and of the holding of the show or obedience trial and of the opportunity to have the dog judged and to win prize money, ribbons, or trophies, I (we) agree to hold this club, its members, directors, governors, officers, agents, superintendents or show secretary, and any employees of the aforementioned parties, harmless from any claim for loss or injury which may be alleged to have been caused directly or indirectly to any person or thing by the act of this dog while in or upon the show or obedience trial premises or grounds or near any entrance thereto, and I (we) personally assume all responsibility and liability for any such claim; and I (we) further agree to hold the aforementioned parties harmless from any claim for loss of this dog by disappearance, theft, death or otherwise, and from any claim for damage or injury to the dog, whether such loss, disappearance, theft, damage, or injury, be caused or alleged to be caused by the negligence of the club or any of the parties aforementioned, or by the negligence of any other person, or any other cause or causes.

INSTRUCTIONS

1. (Variety) If you are entering a dog of a breed in which there are varieties for show purposes, please designate the particular variety you are entering, i. e., Cocker Spaniel (solid color black, ASCOB, parti-color), Beagles (not exceeding 13 in.; over 13 in. but not exceeding 15 in.), Dachshunds (longhaired, smooth, wirehaired), Collies (rough, smooth), Bull Terriers (colored, white), Fox Terriers (smooth, wire), Manchester Terriers (standard, toy), Chihuahuas (smooth coat, long coat), English Toy Spaniels (King Charles and Ruby, Blenheim and Prince Charles), Poodles (toy, miniature, standard).
2. (Dog Show Class) Consult the classification in this premium list. If the dog show class in which you are entering your dog is divided, then, in addition to designating the class, specify the particular division of the class in which you are entering your dog, i. e., age division, color division, weight division.
3. The following categories of dogs may be entered and shown in Best of Breed competition: Dogs that are Champions of Record and dogs which, according to their owners' records, have completed the requirements for a championship, but whose championships are unconfirmed. The showing of unconfirmed Champions in Best of Breed competition is limited to a period of 90 days from the date of the show where the dog completed the requirements for a championship.
4. A dog must be entered in the name of the person who actually owned it at the time entries for a show closed. If a registered dog has been acquired by a new owner it must be entered in the name of its new owner in any show for which entries closed after the date of acquirement, regardless of whether the new owner has received the registration certificate indicating that the dog is recorded in his name. State on entry form whether transfer application has been mailed to A.K.C. (For complete rule refer to Chapter 16, Section 3.)

***JUNIOR SHOWMANSHIP* — If the dog identified on the front of this entry form is entered in Junior Showmanship, please give the following information:**

CLASS SEE DESCRIPTION OF JUNIOR SHOWMANSHIP CLASSES IN THIS PREMIUM LIST.

Open B

NAME OF JUNIOR HANDLER Mary Wuzzle **DATE OF BIRTH** 6/25/60

ADDRESS 506 Harmony Road

CITY East Harmony **STATE** Conn. **ZIP CODE** 06091

If Junior Handler is not the owner of the dog identified on the face of this form, what is the relationship of the Junior Handler to the owner? Daughter

FIGURE 3

And finally, the entry form for Obedience (fig. 3). This is ten months later, and the dog is now a champion. Mary is still handling the dog in JS, but she has been training him and is also entering him in Obedience. This is the dog's first try for a leg in CD, and his Obedience Trial Class box is filled out for Novice A. There is also a Novice B class, and Mary could have entered Bingo there, but she has wisely avoided it.

While Novice B is open for any handler and dog, it is the *only* Novice class that anyone who has already handled a dog to his CD can enter. Thus, the more experienced handlers are in B, and the scoring is usually tougher.

There's also a choice between Open A and Open B classes in the CDX trials. Open A is the best choice for the new CD dog. Since dogs that have already won their CDX or UD degrees can compete in Open B, the new dog doesn't have much chance of placing among the high scorers. Utility has just one class, and here the CDX dogs battle it out with UD dogs for the high scores and top prizes.

So, if you take your dog into Obedience, and it always scores 195 or above when picking up CDX and UD legs, it has a long future ahead of it as a big winner. That won't hurt your bank account, unless you decide to buy and not build display cases to hold all the trophies.

Since the AKC does not have a law prohibiting personal ambition, many young dog fanciers enter their dogs in all three sports at a given show. Since all point shows charge a separate entry fee for breed ring and Obedience, and most shows now have an entry for JS, a triple entry will usually run to twenty dollars or more.

Quite often, you can kiss some of that money good-bye. Dog shows run in accordance with a preannounced schedule that is stuffed into the envelope along with your entry tickets. To cram all of the action into just a few hours, the schedule is always tight, and delays are infrequent.

Thus, if you have entered your collie in the breed ring and JS at the same show, you might discover that collies will be judged in the breed ring at 1:00 P.M., or the precise time that you're due in the JS class. You'll have a few days to decide what's more important to you: your own ego (JS) or championship points for your dog. Whatever your decision, one entry fee has gone down the drain. And if you have also entered Obedience and your class is due to begin at 1:00 P.M., the choice is yours, but more wasted dollars are involved.

If you have the ambition to tackle more than one sport at a time, then the wisest choices are breed ring and JS. So far as your dog is concerned, it's doing the same thing in both rings and is less likely to become confused. This is the system used by most of the dog-loving families who are just getting their feet wet in the dog game. Mother or father takes the dog into the breed ring, and daughter or son takes the dog into JS.

Nonetheless, many of your peers do succeed in working the same dog in both breed ring and Obedience at the same shows. But every so often, the time conflict will occur and a few nonreturnable dollars will fly away.

Succeeding simultaneously in the breed ring and Obedience depends on how smart your dog is. Since it takes much longer to train them for Obedience, dogs become accustomed to sitting at heel position whenever their master comes to a halt. In the breed ring, of course, they never sit. They stay standing at heel whenever their master comes to a halt.

Here at Walden, we've evolved a simple system that helps prevent confusion when a dog is expected to perform brilliantly in both breed and Obedience. It involves three collars—we call it the collar method—and it works this way:

1. Nylon slip collar. This is the dog's customary collar. It is worn night and day when the dog is not being trained.
2. Show lead collar. This is the slip collar attached to the show lead. The dog wears it only when being trained for the breed ring. In your case, your dog should also wear it when it is being trained for JS.
3. Chain (light) choke collar. The dog wears this only when it's being trained for Obedience.

Canine intelligence, of course, is far below your own. But let's assume that your dog's intelligence is on a par with that of a three-year-old child. If you put a bathing suit on children of that age every time you take them swimming, sooner or later they will realize that when they are wearing the bathing suit they are going swimming and not going to church. Call this intelligence or reasoning or association or whatever you like. The point is that it works with both children and dogs. I'm not sure about cats.

With the collar method, then, it is possible to train the average purebred for both the breed ring and Obedience, and to handle the dog in both sports at the same show, schedule permitting. The method has worked for us, it has worked for hundreds of other owners, and it will work for you. Sooner or later, your dog will grasp the general idea that a slip collar means that nothing much is expected of it except loafing and playing, show lead collar means it had better concentrate on gaiting and standing properly, and chain choke collar means it should concentrate on its Obedience lessons.

So if you're ambitious, hop to it. But please have compassion. While it's true that a healthy dog is stronger, pound for pound, than you are, you probably weigh more than your dog. And after a few hours, the noise and confusion and the crowd will tire you. You won't be as full of vim as you were at breakfast.

Long hours at a dog show will tire your dog, too. And when it is tired, it would prefer to crawl into a corner and snooze than go to work. If your dog is in the breed ring at 9:00 A.M. and has to wait until 4:00 P.M. to do its stuff in Obedience, it may not be on its toes for the latter. Don't blame the dog.

So be wise. At your dog's first few shows, anyway, enter it in just one sport. After those shows, you'll be able to judge its condition and decide whether it can take on an extra sport on the same day.

Just don't push. Every dog matures and learns at its own speed. And there's plenty of time. You can handle a dog in the breed ring until it is five or six years old, and in JS and Obedience until it can't trot around anymore.

DOG LOVERS' GRAB BAG

THE THINGS PEOPLE SAY

Dog fanciers may have the wildest imagination of any special-interest group. Oddly, those who seem to know the most, and are the most willing to bend your ear with all sorts of advice, are those who have been around the dog game for only a short time. Most of them have listened to other newcomers and believed everything they've been told.

Once you become a familiar face at dog shows, a great deal of unsolicited advice will come your way. While much of it will be contradictory, and almost all of it will be nonsense, the advisers are usually sincere people who mean to be helpful. There's just no way of avoiding these well-meaning instant experts. It's always best to be polite and listen, and then to forget what you've heard.

While we have remained loyal to Labradors over the years, we have tried other breeds a few times. One of those breeds was the beautiful Samoyed, one of the world's oldest pure breeds and the ancestor of all the other sled dog breeds. My wife started showing one of the Sams, and he was a champion after five shows. But after every one of those shows, my wife came home and informed me that numerous Samoyed lovers told her that the dog could not succeed because of the color of his collar. He was shown in a red

collar, and the experts claimed that a Sam will only strut his stuff in a blue collar. Presumably, no one had informed the experts that all dogs are color blind. Let's hope you receive some better advice.

Remember that it's always best to do your socializing with other dog fanciers *after* your breed has been judged. Otherwise, you run the danger of picking up all sorts of misinformation that may discourage you before the judging begins.

A great deal of this misinformation will concern professional handlers and judges. The informers are usually adults who own your breed and are present to handle their dogs. At least one will tell you that you should have stayed at home because the dogs in competition include a new one handled by a pro, Mary Bloop. "Mary never loses under Judge Euripides," the informer will confide, "and besides, everybody knows they have a thing going in their private lives." It may seem strange to you that the young and beautiful Mary would give a second look at the ancient Judge Euripides, but if the informer is a college president or a prominent banker, you will tend to either believe or half-believe the confidential information. In either case, you'll think the day is lost before it has started, and you won't be on your toes when you enter the ring. You might ask yourself why the informer didn't stay at home.

As in all careers, some professional handlers are better than others. The best win frequently because they handle dogs of only top quality, and they earn upwards of fifty thousand dollars a year. Of course, there are good and bad judges, too, but if they favor the professionals, there's no way of proving it. It's best to assume that the breed judging is on the level.

About half of the adult amateur handlers you'll meet do suspect some degree of collusion between the judges and the professionals. Almost always, these adults haven't worked at handling, or they are not winning with their dogs. Obviously, they are among the dog fanciers to avoid. They hate the professionals

For this little girl,
happiness is owning
a smooth dachshund.

and suspect all the judges, and one wonders why they stay with the dog game.

The people to listen to at dog shows are the veterans in the dog game. They are the breeders, owners, professional handlers and judges who have been around for fifteen or twenty years or more, and most will confess that they don't know everything.

The veterans are found in numbers at every dog show, and there are sure to be a few in your breed. But they don't wear badges proclaiming their status, so it's necessary to scout around and find out who they are. When you find them, make sure they're not busy, introduce yourself, and pop the questions on your mind. Don't debate their answers. You may not agree with them, but it's common courtesy in the dog game to show respect for the veterans. Only veterans argue with veterans.

And only fools argue with judges. Asking questions is okay, so long as the asking takes place outside the show ring. The trick is in finding the judge. When not plying his trade, the average judge prefers solitude to the hazard of facing the owners of losing dogs. Most of their questions are variations of the theme that goes "What didn't you like about my dog?"

"On balance, I liked the winning dog a little better" is the stock answer. It is also the safest, since a judge usually has a hard time remembering the faults of a particular dog. For an enlightening conversation, it's best to ask questions about a breed, rather than a best of a breed.

HEALTH NOTES

If you've been reading carefully, you've already noted that a limping dog is not eligible for any of the dog game's sports. This holds true even if the limp is temporary, such as one caused by a cut pad or a pulled leg muscle.

The reasoning behind the ruling is a canine affliction known as hip dysplasia (HD). It is found in all breeds, although you'll hear that the greyhound is the one exception. Not true. In recent years, HD has popped up in greyhounds, including the racing dogs.

No pup carries HD at birth. It develops over a period of time, and usually it cannot be detected, even by X-ray, before five or six months. What it amounts to is a misfit of the femur head (top of rear leg) in the hip socket. Sometimes, the socket is too shallow to hold the head; or socket or head, or both, have not developed properly.

Mild cases are unimportant, if the dog is kept in proper condition. The dog develops muscles that compensate for any deficiency by holding the femur head in place. The dog does not limp and appears sound. There are millions of mild cases running around, and millions of owners have never heard of HD.

In severe cases, the dog will limp. In very severe cases, the dog has a hard time getting on its feet and drags its rear legs. In both cases, the dog is in pain.

HD has been researched for a long time and several schools of thought exist. Many experts believe that it is hereditary, and they point to the German shepherd as a prime example. Unless the Almighty works a miracle, more than half of that breed's pups whelped this year and in future years will develop HD. In general, the bigger the breed, the more likely the incidence of HD.

Nobody is really sure about the heredity theory. A pup whose parents and grandparents are known to be free of HD can still pop up with the affliction. On the other hand, when either or both sire and dam are known to be HD cases, some or all of their pups will develop into HD-free adults. While the heredity theory remains unproven, wise breeders play it safe and do not breed HD stock. This is one of the best reasons, by the way, for buying a pup from a play-it-safe breeder and not from a pet shop. Sure, you can buy a pup on time payments from a pet shop, but you could also be buying an HD dog. Your vet just can't tell you if the pup is HD-free.

The second school of thought—and it has been developing just recently—is that HD can be induced through improper care and nutrition. While everybody loves a fat, happy pup, it carries too much weight for its soft, growing bones, and this can cause trouble in its hips and bring on HD. The antidote—and this is extremely important in the big breeds—is to keep the growing pup lean. Not fat, not skinny, but lean. The flesh just covers its ribs. So if you own a pup, for heaven's sake don't overfeed it. Unlike a kitten, the average pup will eat until it can hardly waddle.

As for nutrition: Down through the ages, the big myth has been that a dog must have meat. Through massive advertising, the big manufacturers of wet (canned) dog foods have been able to keep this myth alive, mostly through emphasizing the fact that the canine is a carnivorous animal. Well, perhaps the dog was a meat-eater when it was first domesticated, but that was over forty thousand years ago. Today, the dog has adapted itself to human habits, and it's almost as omnivorous as we are—in other words, it will eat just about anything.

The plain truth is that dogs do not need meat. Many of this nation's leading kennels haven't used it in years. The best of the prepared dried foods (moistened before feeding) carry all of the nutritional elements the average dog needs to grow and stay healthy.

Some leading breeders do continue to add a little meat to their dogs' diets, mostly for flavor. In my case, I've avoided meat for flavoring for almost twenty-five years. Meat serves as a laxative for some dogs, and it also contains calcium phosphate. The myth about that is that a pup's growing bones require it. False. Growing bones require calcium *lactate* (in milk and other dairy products, and also available in powder form). As for calcium phosphate, the phosphate negates the calcium, and that's no help to the growing hip sockets and femur heads.

So, I do like to add a little flavoring. Sometimes it's gravy, table scraps, or leftover, cooked vegetables. Otherwise, a few tablespoons of canned fish or chicken, both cheaper and higher in protein count than canned meat, are added to the moistened dry foods. And all of my dogs, now and in the past, have been healthy beasts.

Believe me, I may be a thrifty man, but I don't stay away from canned dog meats just because they are expensive. Take a look at a label one of these days: "Moisture content: 70 percent"—or more. A pretty expensive drink of water, what?

SAFETY NOTES

The deeper you go in the dog game and the more you train your dog, the more valuable it becomes to you—your best friend, and also an investment. But never, never overrate its intelligence. Compared to yours, it doesn't amount to beans.

Your dog cannot safeguard itself at all times. Let it run loose and it's sure to get into trouble, get killed, or join the missing that are never found. Those missing dogs, now close to two million a year, are the backbone of a crime wave known as dognapping. While it doesn't get much publicity, it amounts to the stealing of dogs and the reselling of them to research laboratories and big industry (for safety tests, as in autos). Dognapping is now an organized business, and the big majority of missing dogs are the victims of this business. The canines are usually running loose when they're stolen. No matter where you live in this country, you can't count on your dog being safe. And the criminals prefer to pick up purebreds, of course, since they bring the highest prices. There's both federal and state legislation around to deter the dognappers, but the laws have been ineffective thus far.

So supervise your dog at all times. When you can't be with it, be sure that it's contained. A six-by-twenty-foot outdoor run, with shade and shelter and water provided, is big enough for any dog. A fenced-in yard isn't a good bet. Sooner or later, somebody will come along and forget to shut the gate. Good-bye, dog.

Even a well-trained dog, or one that has been trained to stay within the confines of your property, isn't safe. There are plenty of cases on record of dognappers cleaning out kennels in the absence of the owners. And you can't really put faith in any dog to stay where you've trained it to stay. If the wind is right, the scent of a bitch in season miles away will prove irresistible to a romantic dog, and he'll be off. Or if a couple of dogs start playing across the street, or a cat comes into view, even the well-trained dog might forget its training. And it will be too stupid to know that the man in the approaching truck isn't going to apply the brakes.

ACQUIRING YOUR PUP

For those who are short on cash and can't afford the price of a purebred pup, there are several ways of acquiring one without cost.

The strangest way of all is related to a sad fact of life: every year, at the end of summer, hundreds of thousands of purebred pups and adult dogs are abandoned by their owners. The majority are abandoned in vacation country, when their owners return to the city. And then, in every season of the year, unsupervised pups wander from home, get lost, and sometimes show up at a stranger's back door.

If you find such a stray pup, the proper thing to do is to make every effort to locate its owner: read the lost-and-found columns, place an ad in one, and notify both the police and the nearest humane society. If the owner cannot be found in a month's time, the pup is yours, if you want it.

Let's assume that the stray pup that arrives at your back door is a collie bitch. You make every effort to find her owner, and fail. Meanwhile you've fallen in love with the pup and have decided to keep her. As the pup matures, you realize she's one heck of a good collie, and you want to take her into the dog game. But you don't have her registration certificate. What to do?

This is a problem, all right, but it does have a solution. Write to the AKC, explain your problem, and request the names of authorities on the collie breed in your area. If those authorities agree that the pup is a purebred collie, then the AKC usually grants a listed rather than a registration number. That listed number qualifies your collie for Obedience and Junior Showmanship at the dog shows. The only real drawback is that your dog's pups, if you ever breed her, cannot be registered with the AKC.

A man who really accomplished miracles with a stray pup is my friend Bill Watkins. The pooch was half-starved when he was found by the side of a road. Bill brought the stray home, nursed him back to full health, but couldn't locate the pup's owner. Now, Bill wasn't a dog fancier, knew nothing about the dog game, but he liked the pup and decided to keep him. Bill didn't know anything about training a dog; somebody told him about an obedience school, so he enrolled. The pup proved to be the brightest canine student at the school, and people started urging Bill to have a try at the Obedience trials, something he had never heard of before.

By then it was apparent that the pup was really a standard poodle. Bill went through the procedure with the AKC outlined above and received a listed number for his dog. That dog is Dudley. He's an old man now and retired, but in his heyday Dudley broke all the records for Obedience dogs. It's not likely that any dog of any breed will ever achieve so many perfect (200) scores.

Years before Dudley came into his life, Bill had owned one other dog. He had not been able to train that dog to do a single thing. The team of Bill and his Dudley, then, constitutes a fine testimonial for obedience schools.

Your chances of finding a stray purebred pup, of course, can't be estimated. It can happen tomorrow or never, but another good source for free pups (although a small token fee is often requested) is your nearest humane society shelter. Finding good homes for orphan pups is the main objective of the humane societies, and they often have purebred pups on hand, or might have tomorrow. If the breed you desire isn't available, leave your name and phone number and the society will alert you when the right pup arrives. More often than not, those purebred pups lack either the AKC registration certificate or the litter application form. In such case, here's what to do:

1. Check with the previous owner, if known. Perhaps the pup was registered, or there was a litter application. If so, and the former owner should be willing to sign either form over to you, then your pup is in the clear. It can be registered and entered in the dog shows. If the proper papers are not available, the previous owner may be able to supply you with the registration numbers of the pup's dam and sire and the name of the breeder. Send all information to the AKC. If it checks out, your new pup will be registered and will be qualified for all three of the dog game's sports. Otherwise:
2. Proceed as with the stray pup, and apply for a listed number. Officially, this is known as an Indefinite Listing Privilege, or an ILP, number. Again, this is good for Obedience only, not the breed ring. If entered in Obedience, of course, the ILP dog can also go into JS.

Although dog breeding is an exact science, nature has a way of fooling the best of the canine experts, and that's why, when a purebred pup's pedigree is unknown, the AKC will often list a pup but not register him. If listed, the pup can't be shown in the breed ring or used for breeding. While this may sound silly, consider the following true tale:

Years ago, I sold a yellow, male Labrador puppy to a man who already owned an adult Chesapeake Bay retriever bitch. A couple of years later, the dog and the bitch enjoyed an unplanned mating. All of the seven pups in the resultant litter were black. From the moment they were whelped and all through their adulthoods, every pup looked like a Labrador. Although it was a mixed breeding, not a single member of that litter showed any evidence that its dam was a Chesapeake.

You can be sure, however, that the dam's genes wouldn't have stayed hidden forever. If a dog of that litter had been bred to a Labrador bitch, at least some of those pups would have looked like mixed breeds. So glory to the AKC for not taking any chances. Nature works in mysterious ways.

Of course, the best source for a purebred, registered pup is always a veteran breeder. If you can't locate the right one in your area, drop a note to Breeders' Aid at the AKC requesting the names of nearby breeders of collies, Saint Bernards, beagles, or whatever. Within a couple of weeks, the AKC will respond with the needed information.

Unfortunately, most breeders do not give away their pups. While prices vary in different parts of the country, purebred pups in almost all breeds bring a minimum of one hundred dollars. Incidentally, that's just about what it costs to raise a pup to the age of eight weeks, when it's ready for its new home. And maybe you'll be surprised to learn that purebred puppy prices haven't increased much over the past forty years. The price of everything else has soared, including the price of dog food, but not purebred puppy prices.

It is always best not to trust those breeders who claim they don't have the pup's papers on hand, but they'll send them along to you. A legitimate breeder will either sign and turn over to you the pup's AKC registration certificate or the pup's AKC litter application form.

To understand the latter, here's how it works:

1. When the pups are whelped, the breeder applies for a litter registration. The AKC then supplies the proper number of litter forms, or one for each pup.

2. Each form is marked male or female. This, properly signed by the breeder and you, is mailed to the AKC. If you enclose the proper amount (three dollars), the AKC will send you the pup's individual registration certificate. You name the pup.

If the pup is already individually registered, the certificate, properly signed, is sent along to the AKC with two dollars, and change of ownership is duly recorded. In this case, the pup has already been named. There's nothing you can do about that, but there's no law that says you must call the pup by that name. Plain old Bill is a better name for a dog than Percy of Starlight Hill.

A purchased pup is not a free pup, of course, but it is free as far as you are concerned if it arrives as a birthday or Christmas present. To achieve this end, it is usually necessary to wage a campaign with one's parents.

Repeating the phrase "I want a puppy" three times a day over a six-month period is seldom enough, unless your parents are accustomed to giving you anything you desire. Usually, it is necessary to organize a campaign and employ indisputable logic. If you pledge to take complete responsibility for the pup, then the battle is half-won. I've never heard of parents who didn't want their children to be responsible, and that's something that isn't always learned in school. And if you can get your parents to think about it, dog shows will teach you poise and sportsmanship as well as how to get along with complete strangers.

Sometimes, of course, one has to compromise to achieve one's desire. The daughter of friends of mine didn't get her pup until she took the pledge to take piano lessons, something she had been avoiding for years. Sally is now an accomplished pianist and a great success in the dog game. She's happy, and so are her parents. Of course, your parents might not be so demanding. Maybe all you'll have to do to get your pup is to swear on a stack of Bibles that you'll mow the lawn every week.

Since dog shows are designed for the improvement of the purebreds, there's no place at them for the mixed breeds (mongrels). Still, if you own a mixed breed, there's no harm in training it. It will be a worthwhile experience for you, and a beneficial one for

the dog. A trained dog is always a better pet than an untrained one.

Almost all of the obedience schools welcome the mixed breeds, and many of them hold Obedience trials for their canine graduates. The same goes for the 4-H Clubs. And then there are the pet shows, usually staged to raise money for animal welfare or some other charity. Nobody knows how many pet shows are held annually, but it's a cinch that there are more pet shows than dog shows. They are always fun for both you and your dog, and worth entering—even if you just have your mind set on picking up a few prizes. Finding the pet shows is usually a matter of keeping your eyes peeled for announcements in your local newspapers.

One of the great myths of the dog game—and you are bound to hear it sooner or later—is that a show dog cannot succeed if it is also a house pet. The theory seems to be that the house pet is always a lazy, spoiled beast that can't find the pep to win in the breed ring and Obedience.

Well, this is a bunch of hot air. Better than 90 percent of the successful dogs in the breed competition and Obedience are also house pets. Still, the myth just won't fade away, and I have an idea that it is perpetuated by the professional handlers who like to keep their clients' dogs with them all the time. This, of course, brings in extra money for boarding—several dollars a day per dog, although it costs only pennies a day to feed a dog.

So believe this: The show dog doesn't have to live in a kennel. And the vast majority don't. If your dog has the right conformation, it will win its championship in the breed ring whether it sleeps on or under your bed. If it has average canine intelligence, and you can bring this intelligence out through training, sleeping on the sofa won't hinder its chances of winning the Obedience degrees. And even if it is a very foolish, spoiled dog, you can win with it in JS. My own winners have always been house dogs.

There's a lesson to be learned from the army of adult dog fanciers who just can't wait until their purebred pups are six

Even parents might find it hard to resist this little Scottish terrier puppy.

months old, the magic age for eligibility in the breed ring. As soon as the pups are old enough, they are rushed into Puppy Class. The individual owners, of course, hope their pups will take the blue ribbon in that class and then go on to Winners Dog and pick up a few championship points. Unless the pup belongs to one of the toy breeds, which mature very early, its owner is a dreamer. In all other breeds, a young pup stands about as much chance of winning championship points as a seven-year-old girl stands of winning the Miss America contest.

While the dreamers realize this, they rationalize that the pup, even as a sure loser, is picking up valuable experience for the future. This is true to the extent that the pup does get used to what's expected of it in the breed ring, and it does become accustomed to the strange sounds and scents of a dog show, and become less confused (as time goes on) over the plenitude of other dogs and people. However, while gaining this experience the pup is eating up a tidy sum in entry fees, as well as padding the entries. The more dogs present in the breed, the more the championship points for the lucky adult dog that proves to be the winner.

More often than not, the young pup is wasting both its owner's time and money. Not even breeders who know their bloodlines well can accurately predict that a pup that looks like a winner at six months will develop into a winner at a year. The pup may develop into a bum as a young adult and stand absolutely no chance of winning over the mature dogs it must challenge.

In the medium-sized and large breeds, it is always best to wait until a pup has done its maximum growing before entering it in the breed ring. If the pup looks close to its breed standard at ten months, then you have a budding champion on your hands. Chances are that it's going to improve and not go downhill.

What to do with a pup before it's ten months old? Well, there's always JS, where it will pick up what amounts to breed ring experience. Better still, there's Obedience. True, the training is more difficult, but you'll end up with a better-trained dog. If you take your dog into the trials, you'll have plenty of time to study its cousins in the breed ring, compare it with the best, and decide whether it has the quality to harvest a crop of championship points.

Make sense? If not, consider this fact: Physically, a dog enjoys its best years (prime condition) between one and six. That gives it five years of breed ring competition. So it has plenty of time to make a record for itself as a winner of breed ring, group, and Best-in-Show trophies.

Now, the above advice conflicts with that of most dog fanciers. They will argue that an Obedience dog doesn't show well in the breed ring, although the record books are full of evidence to the contrary. Show me a person who puts breed ring before Obedience for a pup, and I'll show you a lazy dog fancier.

That's the way I do things these days: Obedience first. The AKC will not fine you if you disagree, but I've found that my way makes the best sense. And it is always the very best course to take in the case of a stubborn or difficult pup. Those pups do come along now and then, but training will turn them into proper canine citizens.

Once a dog has won its championship or a particular Obedience degree, the AKC—keeper of the records—sends (gratis) a certificate that resembles a diploma to the dog's owner. The championship one measures nine by twelve inches, while the Obedience one measures only six by nine inches. Does this mean that the AKC believes that beauty is a more valuable canine quality than brains? Nobody knows.

The AKC does not award diplomas or anything else to junior handlers who achieve outstanding success in Junior Showmanship. If you think that's being unfair to mortals, write to your senators.

THE WESTMINSTER KENNEL CLUB
96th Annual Dog Show
1972
1972 THE WESTMINSTER KENNEL CLUB 1972

THE WELL-READ DOG LOVER

The dog game's most important address does not belong to the White House. It belongs to the American Kennel Club: 51 Madison Avenue, New York, New York 10010. The nonprofit organization was founded in 1884 for "the advancement of purebred dogs" and has been doing just that ever since. It is the governing body of American dogdom and employs both a small army of people and several computers to keep reasonably up-to-date.

If you are already in or headed into the dog game, write to the AKC for single, free copies of one or all of the following booklets: *Rules Applying to Registration and Dog Shows* (breed ring), *Regulations for Junior Showmanship,* and *Obedience Regulations.*

The nitty gritty of all you should know about the dog game's sports is included in those publications, including small things that might not cross your mind. For example, a bitch in season, even if entered in a show, should be left at home. Obviously, she

This Labrador retreiver wanted to make sure he knew all the rules before entering a recent show at the Westminster Kennel Club.

would distract the attention of male dogs at the show, and might even cause some unavoidable dog fights. Thus, such a bitch cannot enter Obedience.

While the AKC cannot send you to jail for defying its rules and regulations, it might levy a fine or remove your privileges, so that you can't be active for six months or so. It is probably true that a few people do break the rules and get away with it at every show, but this isn't cricket, and not even the dogs appreciate it.

As you move along in the dog game, you are almost sure to acquire a personal library of canine-oriented books. Scores of new ones are published every year, and a good way to go broke is to buy all of them. Fortunately, it's possible to be a well-read dog lover without investing a fortune.

The big majority of the books (old and new) are devoted to just one breed. Dog fanciers call them breed books, although authors and publishers prefer to think of them as breed bibles. As any veteran will tell you, breed books rate all the way from horrible to excellent, and often an old one is superior to the very newest on a given breed. A little literary research is recommended. Ask a few old-timers in your favorite breed about the breed bibles they favor. For balance, most will name one American and one British breed book. The British books seem to have an edge on quality, but don't take the English breed standard to heart. The American breed standard is often a little different, and it's the one that really counts on this side of the Atlantic.

There are also a few multiple-breed books, each designed to cover several related or similar (in purpose) breeds. My only contribution in this area is *Those Lovable Retrievers* (McGraw-Hill, 1973), covering the seven retriever breeds found in America and including advice from the top authorities on each. And then, for all the recognized breeds, there's *The Complete Dog Book,* the official tome of the AKC. Short histories and full breed standards are included, but not for the miscellaneous breeds. The books one must go to for full coverage (recognized, miscellaneous, and rare breeds) are the various dog encyclopedias. Almost all give the breed standards short treatment, and all are big, heavy, and expensive. Only the one published by Stackpole offers complete breed standards.

If you are headed for the breed ring, you'll find valuable tips on handling, grooming, and what to anticipate, in *Your Show Dog* by Maxwell Riddle (Doubleday, 1968). And one of the best of the many books on Obedience is *Expert Obedience Training for Dogs* by Winfred G. Strickland (Macmillan, 1968). And let's not forget *The Pleasures of Dog Ownership* (Prentice-Hall, 1971), the only book around providing an in-depth look at all facets of the dog show world, with advice from leading dog fanciers, judges, handlers, and breeders. I happen to be very high on that book. Maybe because my wife and I coauthored it.

Often, it's difficult to find the dog book you're looking for in the local bookstore. This is not because booksellers hate dogs. No bookstore in this land can possibly stock all of the forty thousand new books (fiction and nonfiction) published in this country every year. Nor can any library.

While any bookstore can order a book for you, some consider it too much trouble. If you can't find a cooperative store, you can always order any book from its publisher. Just write to the sales department and include title of book and author's name, plus a check or money order in the proper amount. If you don't have it, your librarian can supply you with the publisher's address.

Should your literary interest develop to the point where you start searching for hard-to-find old dog-books, the place to write is The Old Dragon Book Den, Box 186, Barrington, Illinois 60010. The Old Dragon offers used, old, and rare dog-books, and is a favorite haunt of book collectors.

Now, it's not always necessary to pay the full price for a dog book that you want, and especially one that was published a few years ago. If you have the time, you can always shop around at secondhand bookstores, tag sales, church and charity book sales, and private auctions. It so happens that I'm a collector, although not just of dog books. Over the years, I've saved a small fortune by shopping around and keeping my eyes open. Rest assured that they were wide open when I paid less than a dollar for a very old English dog book that I knew was worth at least two hundred dollars. I found it at a tag sale in a garage. Somebody had cleaned out his attic and thought he was selling a lot of junk. I assumed the person was a cat lover.

A few hardy dog fanciers collect and sell dog books, but only as a sideline. It's not the way to make a living. Still, there are many ways to make money (part or full time) in the dog game, and you don't have to be of voting age to start. A love for dogs is the main qualification. However, that's another book, it's called *How to Make Money in Dogs* (Dodd, Mead, 1974), and it's one of mine.

Once you start collecting dog books, it is necessary to put a ban on borrowing. I learned this the hard way. The dog lover who borrows a book from you is almost sure to lend it to another dog lover, and that happens again and again until nobody remembers who has the book, and the person who has it doesn't confess. These days, if a friendly dog lover wants to read a book on my shelf, he reads it under my roof. So don't even trust your Pekingese-loving Aunt Tillie, even if she does promise to put you in her will. You can be sure that she has Pekingese-loving friends who will want to borrow the book.

Most dog fanciers subscribe to a canine journal or two. Many of the publications are devoted to just one breed, and are available by subscription only from the appropriate national breed club. A sampling: *Afghan International, American Chow Chow, Boxer Review, Cocker Spaniel Visitor, Dane Dispatch, German Short-haired Pointer, Italian Greyhound, Shih Tzu News, Shetland Sheepdog, Top Dobe, Bobtail Express,* and *Poodle Review*.

And then there are several national magazines devoted to coverage of all the breeds and the many facets of the dog game. These are the best bets:

Pure-Bred Dogs—American Kennel Gazette. The official AKC publication, and the only canine journal to publish complete records of licensed show, Obedience trial, and JS winners. Also features breed columns, show dates, list of member clubs, breeders, AKC doings, and general articles. For the serious students of the dog game. Same address as AKC. Subscription only.

Dogs. The biggie (in circulation) of the world's canine journals, with articles devoted to the breeds, canine research, related legislation, news from the veterinary world, stamp collecting, and book reviews. For just plain dog lovers and dog fanciers. Address: 257 Park Avenue South, New York, New York 10010. By subscription and on most newsstands.

While one or two of the above should keep anyone current in the dog game, some ardent dog fanciers devote all of their reading time to numerous canine magazines. They read those already named, plus the likes of *Kennel Review, Dogs in Canada, Hunting Dog, Dog World,* and *The American Field.* Check with your nearest ardent dog fancier or librarian for addresses and subscription rates.

No matter your breed and whatever your particular interests in the dog game, you'll find plenty of reading material. Just don't let the reading interfere with your studying. Dogs are great, but a solid education is more important. Always. Really.

Time now to wish the best of everything to you and your dog. Once the two of you succeed as a team in the dog game, your dog will wear its fame lightly, but you'll have to remember to keep your feet on the ground. Your new halo will not mean that you can fly.

GLOSSARY OF SHOW TERMS

Adult dog	One year or older, either sex.
All 'rounder	A person licensed to judge all breeds.
American-bred	Dog whelped in the United States out of dam bred in the United States.
American Kennel Club	Governing body of U.S. dogdom.
Benched show	Show where dogs must remain on display for a specified period.
Best in Show	Top dog at given point show.
Bitch	Female canine, any age.
Bite:	Where dog's upper and lower incisors meet.
Level	Even, exactly edge to edge.
Overshot	Uppers overlap.
Scissors	Lowers touch insides of uppers.
Undershot	Lowers protrude beyond uppers.
Blaze	Splash of white running up muzzle.
Blooded	Purebred.
Bloom	Gloss of coat.
Brace	Two dogs of same breed; look-alikes.
Breed	Dog of specified type.
Recognized	Registered by the AKC.
Miscellaneous	Listed by the AKC.
Breed ring	Where a dog wins its championship.

Bum	Dog with slight resemblance to its breed.
Catalog	Dog show publication giving details: dogs, owners, judges, events, prizes, etc. Available at every show.
CD	Companion Dog.
CDX	Companion Dog Excellent.
Champion	Breed titleholder.
Character	Desired personality of a breed.
Clip	In some breeds (poodle, terrier) coat is clipped to meet breed standard requirements.
Crabbing	When gaiting, dog angles in and crowds handler. Improper.
Cropping	In some breeds (boxer, bouvier) ears are trimmed to make them stand erect and conform with breed standards.
Crossbreed	Result of mating between two different breeds.
Cryptorchid	Male lacking both testicles; ineligible for breed ring.
Dam	A pup's mother.
Dewclaw	Useless fifth toe, not common to all breeds.
Distemper	Most common infectious disease.
Docking	Shortening natural tail of some breeds (airedale, fox terrier).
Dog	Generally, any canine; specifically, a male.
Dog show	Where the action is in the dog game.
Down-faced	Muzzle slants downward from skull to nose tip.
Dropper	Pointer-setter crossbreed.
Dudley nose	Flesh-colored nose.
Ears:	Ears are ears.
Bat	Erect, broad at base, and rounded.
Drop	Hang and fall forward.
Flying	Extended, look like wings.
Natural	As nature intended.

Pricked	Upright.
Rose	Small and fold backward.
Semipricked	Upright but tips lean forward.
Tulip	Carried up and forward.
Entry form	Contract between dog show and dog's owner.
Expression	Desired head, ears, eyes, and spirit for breed.
Fall	Long hairs fall over and hide face (English sheepdog).
Feather	Hair fringe on back of legs, bottom of tail (English setter).
Fiddle head	Long, narrow head.
Finished	A champion; has finished collecting its points.
Flews	Pendulous upper lips (at corners).
Foreface	Muzzle.
Foul color	Undesirable color for breed.
Gait	Dog's natural trot.
Grooming	Proper care of canine coat.
Grizzle	Bluish-gray coat color.
Hackles	Hair on back of neck stands up when dog is excited.
Handler	Person handling a dog, amateur or professional.
Harlequin	A color combination (black on white).
Heat	In season—bitch's period for breeding.
Height	Measured from withers to ground.
Hepatitis	A serious liver disease.
Inbreeding	Mating closely related dogs; always a gamble.
Incisors	Upper and lower front teeth.
Judge	Loved or unloved person, either sex, who makes final decisions at dog shows.
Kennel blind	You, when you refuse to recognize your dog's faults.
Kink tail	Sharply bent or broken.
Kisses	Tan spots over eyes and on cheeks.
Layback	Slope of shoulder.

LEAD	Leash; also *Liam.*
LEATHER	Flap of ear.
LEPTOSPIROSIS	A serious kidney disease.
LITTER	Pups of same whelping.
LUMBER	Excess poundage.
MANTLE	Coat is darker over shoulder, back, and sides.
MASK	Dark shading on muzzle.
MATCH	An informal dog show.
MERLE	Blue, gray, and black coat.
MONGREL	Dog of mixed-breed parents.
MONORCHID	One testicle missing; not eligible for breed ring.
MUZZLE	Foreface of dog.
PACING	Legs on one side move in unison.
PARTI-COLOR	Coat carries more than one color.
PEDIGREE	Written record of any dog's family tree, including a mongrel's.
PILE	Dense undercoat of soft hair.
POMPON	Rounded tuft at end of tail (poodle).
PREMIUM LIST	Advance notice of dog show, carrying all details.
PUPPY	Under a year.
PUREBRED	A dog whose sire and dam are of the same breed, and whose family tree has always been the same breed.
PUT DOWN	Properly groomed and prepared for the breed ring.
RACY	Tall and slight in conformation.
RINGERS	Dogs that are look-alikes.
RUDDER	Tail.
RUFF	Thick growth of hair around neck.
SADDLE	Darker coat over back.
SELF-COLOR	Solid color, or with shadings.
SIRE	A pup's father.
SOUND	As in "Sound as a rock."
SPAYING	Surgery to prevent bitch from conceiving.
STOP	Angle from muzzle to skull.

TAIL:	Appendage at end of dog's spine.
CRANK	Carried down with tip up; looks like a crank.
GAY	Upright and displayed in gay manner.
PLUME	Greatly feathered.
KINK	Bent or broken.
OTTER	Thick at base, then tapering.
RING	Up and over; almost a circle.
SCREW	Short and spiral.
SICKLE	Out and up in a semicircle.
SQUIRREL	A modified ring tail.
SABER	Similar to the otter, but tip up.
TD	Tracking dog.
TEAM	Four dogs of same breed.
TIMBER	Good leg bone.
TOPKNOT	Tuft of longer hair atop head.
TRICOLOR	Coat color combination of white, black, and tan.
TYPEY	A dog close to its breed's standard.
UD	Utility Dog.
UDT	Utility Dog Tracking.
VARMINTY	The expression of a wise fox.
WEEDY	The dog is too light-boned.
WHELPS	Unweaned pups.
WITHERS	High point of shoulders, right behind neck.
WRINKLES	Loose, folding skin on head and muzzle (bloodhound).

Every country has its own dog game terminology. Much of ours originated in England, where the sport of purebred dogs was popular long before it gained a foothold in this country. While some of the English terms have not caught on in the United States, they are occasionally used by somebody who has just imported a dog from England. In the owner's mind, the dog and the terms add up to a mysterious status. Here's a sampling of a few English terms that you might hear at the dog shows from time to time:

Bred in the purple	A dog of superior breeding.
Bucking about	A high-strung dog; one that jumps about on lead.
Dolling up	Our "Put down."
Gig lamps	Huge, protruding eyes.
Harking a bit	Prick ears.
Knitting a jumper	Dog crosses front legs when gaiting.
Mincing along	Dog takes tiny steps when gaiting.
Mossy-topped	Having a soft coat.
Shelly	A dog in poor condition.
Switchback	Uneven topline.
Titty-faced	Thin foreface.
Upstanding	Excellent reach of neck.

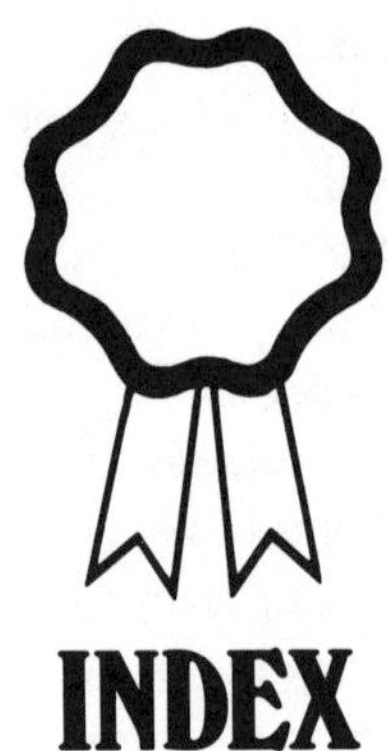

INDEX